Why Yc

# Forgive
# Your Parents

## And How to Do It
## With Ease and Grace

## COLIN TIPPING

### ANA HOLUB
### JULIE JONES
### MEGAN O'CONNOR
### BELLA ROSE FONTAINE

Global 13 Publications, Inc

*Why You Still Need to*
## Forgive Your Parents
*And How To Do It With Ease and Grace*

Date of Publication: May, 2010

**ISBN 978-0-9821790-0-0**

Global 13 Publications, Inc.
26 Briar Gate Lane
Marietta, GA 30066
sales@radicalforgiveness.com

Printed in the United States of America

**Web Site:**        **www.forgivingyourparents.com**
                **www.radicalforgiveness.com**

**Editor:** Nina Amir

This book is dedicated to the two wonderful people
who agreed to my request to be
incarnated through them
and to be my parents:

**Albert Charles Tipping**
and
**Hilda Adelaide Tipping**

# Acknowledgements

My sincere thanks and admiration go to Nina Amir, our editor-in-chief who agreed to look over all the submitted essays, offer kind words and advice to their creators and work one-on-one with those who wanted to bring their submissions up to an acceptable standard. Her four-week writing course by teleconference helped many people improve their skills and encouraged people to keep on writing.

I also want to acknowledge those writers who made a great effort to submit an essay and yet did not quite make the grade for inclusion in this book. So many of them wrote to me and said that even though they had let go of the goal of becoming a co-author, they had found the exercise of writing their stories about forgiving their parents an incredibly healing experience.

I am very pleased to be providing the vehicle for the four people who have co-authored this book with me and I fully acknowledge and appreciate their willingness to share their personal stories with the reader in a way that illustrates the power of Radical Forgiveness to heal our lives. In doing this they offer the readers the opportunity to look at their own lives through the eyes of these writers and to gain insights for themselves. I am confident that those who read these stories will look at how they might too look within themselves and find forgiveness for their parents.

Colin Tipping

# Contents

# Introduction

My wife, JoAnn, and myself have been teaching people how to forgive themselves and others since the late 80s, slowly developing all through the 90s, the method that has now come to be known as Radical Forgiveness. While intending to bring emotional and spiritual healing to cancer patients at the retreats we ran in the North Georgia mountains, we knew we had to find a way of teaching them to heal through forgiveness. But it had to be a lot easier and quicker than anything conventional forgiveness had to offer.

That was when Radical Forgiveness was born. I wrote the book, *Radical Forgiveness: Making Room for the Miracle* in 1997 and began regular workshops in early 1998 and have been doing them around the world ever since.

Having now done hundreds of these workshops I have come to the realization that the vast majority of the problems we have in our lives, and the personal issues we struggle with so desperately all through our adult lives, have their origins in how we were treated by our parents in our early years. This is not to imply that our parents

1

were bad people. Not at all — (or shall we say 'not necessarily' because some parents do, in fact, earn the right to be judged as bad).

Nevertheless, the fact is the majority of parents are just good, ordinary folk, but when we are very young and unable to understand how adults think and behave, we are easily wounded by what they say and do, or by what they don't say and fail to do. These wounds sometimes never heal and become the internal gyroscopes that determine how we create our adult lives, moment by moment — that is, until we heal them.

We shall be examining in the ensuing pages the metaphysical explanation for why this happens to be universally true for virtually everyone, and what spiritual purpose it serves. For now, though, the important thing to know is that our unresolved childhood wounds inevitably get acted out in many ways during our adult life, often times in very destructive ways and very much to our detriment. Destructive, that is, to our careers, our marriages, our social lives and so on.

It is the repressed pain of unresolved childhood wounds that underlie the majority of addictions as well as cause many illnesses like cancer. (We studied the literature on this when we were doing the cancer retreats.) These wounds also get acted out most aggressively in our relationships, and mostly account for why marriages fail, and why people repeatedly create chaos, and apparently dysfunctional relationships throughout their lives.

It seems obvious, therefore, that the most sensible and efficient way to heal our lives and bring more peace and happiness into our existence is to go to the very source of our pain — our parents — and forgive them. Forgive them profoundly, once and for all, for all the things they did, intentionally or unintentionally, that caused us to feel victimized.

How do you know what to forgive them for if the wounds are in our subconscious and. therefore. out of our awareness? That's easy. Look at your life now and see what you are creating in your life that might reflect the beliefs you have about yourself and life in general — especially those that keep you limited and stuck. And who taught you those? Your parents, of course. They didn't know it, any more than you are aware of imparting such subtle teachings to your own children, assuming you are a parent yourself. They were doing the best they could given the knowledge and resources they had, just like you are now.

In Part One of this book I develop this theme and propose a form of forgiveness that you will find to be extremely effective, simple and easy to do. Radical Forgiveness.

However, I believe in the power of story to teach, so when I thought about doing this book, I invited people who had a story to tell and liked to write, to co-author this book with me. I asked them to write a chapter that would show how Radical Forgiveness had enabled them to forgive one or both parents, or for that matter, grandparents or stepparents. *[Note: We are using the term parents generically to possibly include grandparents, uncles, aunts and step parents where this is applicable.]*

Part Two of the book, therefore, contains their essays, and I hope you enjoy the stories they have to tell. I am very grateful for their willingness to participate and I trust that their efforts will be rewarded in the ways that mine have been. I have found in my late-breaking career that the greatest reward comes in knowing that you have changed someone's life for the better. I have no doubt that their contributions will do just that for a lot of people.

I also know that the process of writing their own stories have been both cathartic and healing for them at a very deep level, and for that reason alone it has been a challenge. However, when people are able to truly forgive their parents for beating them, abandoning them, sexually abusing them, or wounding them in some other way when they were children, it is big — very big. It is nothing less than heroic.

Enjoy the book and let it be the catalyst that begins a healing between you and your parents, no matter whether they are still on this side of life or not.

# 1: God Makes No Mistakes

## By Colin Tipping

*"I hate my Mother!"* Gwen growled, glaring into the distance across the large square cushion she was kneeling in front of, as if her mother was right there. The tennis racquet which she had just used to beat that cushion with remained poised in her hands, ready for more — a lot more. It was like she was in a trance, replaying her experience in her mind, remembering and feeling the incredible rage she had bottled up over the years. Her lips were drawn tight, her eyes glaring and her entire body was trembling.

"Why do you hate her, Gwen? I asked very quietly.

*"Because she didn't love me!"* she shouted and immediately sprang back into action, bringing the racquet back over her head and thrashing that cushion as energetically as she possibly could, over and over again until she collapsed from total exhaustion, her head on the cushion, her body curled over, panting. After a few seconds, she began to sob. Softly at first but then loud anguished sobs that came from somewhere deep down in her body and from the furthest recesses of her mind. It was clearly

5

very old pain. It had to be — Gwen was 92 years of age. She was, to date, the most senior person I have ever had at one of my workshops and one of the most courageous. I just rubbed her back and comforted her for several minutes without saying anything. The sobbing eased off and for a few moments she was completely still, virtually catatonic. I wasn't sure what was happening within her, so I took my hands off her and just watched. She was still curled over the cushion with her head buried in her lap, but suddenly her whole body shook quite violently for a couple of seconds, just like a dog shakes its body after coming out of a lake.

I heard a strange muffled sound coming from her mouth that, for a moment or two I couldn't identify. Then I realized. She was laughing. She rolled over and continued laughing quite hysterically for quite a time as if she had seen the point of a great joke and couldn't stop laughing at it. It was a joyful laughter. Everyone else in the room began to laugh with her and moved closer.

"I just got it!" she spluttered, still laughing. "She wasn't *able* to love me." Pausing to get her breath she blurted out — "She didn't have it in her . . . . the poor woman didn't know how to love . . . . . . She didn't even love herself. . . . . she hated herself, poor thing. How could she possibly have loved me?"

Suddenly the laughing stopped as quickly as it had begun. The sadness suddenly took over and she began crying softly.

"Colin, I've spent my whole life demanding that she give me what she was unable to give and blaming her for my pain. And, it wasn't her fault. She loved me in the only way she could."

"That's exactly right, Gwen." I said. "And you've carried that pain for almost 90 years, haven't you?"

"Yes."

"What effect do you think that has had on your life? Have other people you loved rejected you in the same way or similar?" There was a pause. She was thinking.

"Wow!" Gwen looked up at me, with eyes wide. "The lightbulb just went on," she said. "How ridiculous is this? I've spent my whole life attracting people into my life who I thought really didn't love me. In all their different ways, they did exactly what my mother did to me. Rejected me. My first husband was quite affectionate and caring and we got along fine for 12 years, but he eventually left. He couldn't take my jealousy and neediness. I was so demanding. He just couldn't give me what I wanted, he said, and left."

"That's because you wouldn't let him," I said. "You wouldn't let anyone love you because it didn't fit your story."

"What story?" she asked.

"The one you made up as a result of your feeling unloved by your mother," I replied. "You decided right then that you must be unlovable. And you've held that belief your whole life, haven't you?"

7

"That's right, I've always felt that I didn't measure up or was never good enough. I spent all my time trying to prove that I was enough and trying to get people to love me. But it didn't work."

"Look, Gwen, your story is not entirely untrue," I said. "Your mother really did reject you. and it hurt, right?" Looking back, you have to admit, she treated you very badly, didn't she?" Gwen nodded.

"That's right, and no one is going to say you are not entitled to feel that pain. We all want to be loved, especially by our mothers. But as any child would, instead of seeing it being about her and her inability to love, you thought there must be something wrong with you; that you were not OK; that you must be unlovable. Over time you elevated that to a belief, and that belief has run your life."

There was a long pause. She lowered her head but stared at the cushion that a few moments ago had been the container for her rage. After about a minute she raised her head turned towards me.

"What do I do now, then?" she asked quizzically.

"Give up the need to have your mother love you," I replied quickly. "It's your need for her love and approval that keeps you stuck because she can never give it to you! Needing it disempowers you. You can never be free until you give up the need."

I then put the tennis racquet back in her hand and told her to hit the cushion again, just like she did when she was being rageful, but this time she was to say in a very loud voice, with each stroke, *"I give up my need for my mother to love me. I am lovable already, and I am open to receive love now."* She pounded it in about ten times.

Upon completion of that process, she looked triumphant and simply glowed. The group applauded loudly and brought her the center of the room and laid her on a blanket. We played her a song called *"How Could Anyone Ever Tell You That You Are Anything Less Than Beautiful,"* sung by LaWanda Badger, one of our RF coaches. She had some tears, but all the sadness had vanished. They were simply tears of joy.

This was not the end of the process by any means. She was on the way to forgiving her mother with Radical Forgiveness, but there was more to go yet. She had done the first two of the five stages to Radical Forgiveness and some of Stage Three, but that was it. I will explain later what those five stages are and tell you then what I asked Gwen to do next.

The point I want to make here, and the reason why I opened with this true story (I swear to you that it really did happen though Gwen was not her real name), is that it proves it is never too late to forgive your parents. For a few moments I saw this 92 year old lady become a small child again. She touched into some pain that she had buried almost 90 years prior, but pain that she had acted out all through her whole life without her knowing it.

You might ask, what's the point when you are that age? Why not let sleeping dogs lie? Why rake up the past? Her parents were obviously long gone anyway, so what difference would it make? Well, I can tell you, it made a huge difference to her. She may have been 92, but this woman was full of life and had plenty of reasons in her mind to find peace with her own parents before she died. She knew that her own death was more likely to be peaceful and pain free if she passed without a whole lot of repressed rage in her body.

What she didn't realize at the time, though, but came to appreciate soon afterwards was that she had 'infected' her own children with the same energy. They were carrying her pain in their own energy field, particularly her daughter. She, too, was playing it out by also creating relationships where love was both withheld and not received.

By doing the Radical Forgiveness process on her parents, which works by collapsing energy fields built up around such issues as she had, she was collapsing the energy field that her children were carrying too. She was releasing them from the need to carry her pain any longer. It was a huge gift to them, and Gwen didn't realize it until that moment. The children didn't realize it either and probably still don't. But I would nevertheless wager that their lives changed from that point on and that they found it easier to receive love. That's how it works with Radical Forgiveness.

The other thing that is demonstrated by this story is that sleeping dogs don't lie. They play dead for a while perhaps, but sooner or later they will try to come to the surface. Everyone has an inbuilt urge to heal themselves so any trauma or wound that is not worked through at the time with all associated feelings repressed, will find a way to come to the surface to be healed. This will manifest in a number of ways, not always obvious, of course, least of all to the person experiencing it. Gwen's pattern of unconsciously choosing partners who would consistently reject her and make her feel unlovable is a perfect example. She was replaying the original wound each time while at the same time confirming and exposing her core-negative belief that she was unlovable.

By way of another example of this, one woman whose name was Ellen and was an attendee at one of my workshops told me she was about to lose her job. "Don't worry," she said. "It happens to me all the time. No matter what job I get, it always disappears after about three years. Either I get fired, or the firm goes down or something occurs where I have to move on. I know there has to be a reason for it, but I don't know what it is."

She was right. There was a reason. It turned out that when she was age three her father died. As a result of his sudden and unexpected death, her mother had a mental breakdown and had to go into a treatment center. Consequently, Ellen was put with the grandparents who, it transpired, were not kind people. They mistreated her mentally and emotionally and were not above using physical abuse as a way to punish her.

In her own mind she saw herself as having been *abandoned* by her parents, and that they had left her with grumpy old grandparents who were cruel and nasty. Up to that point she had been happy and content. Her parents had been kind and loving, and life had been good. And now, at age three, it become almost unbearable and as far as she was concerned her parents were the ones to blame. It was all their fault.

Because of her experience and her perception of what happened to her at age three, her subconscious mind took hold of that number and by association, linked it to breakdown and abandonment. You need to understand that the subconscious mind is not a reasoning mind; it thinks only in very simple terms, mostly by association. Ellen's subconscious mind formed the idea that based on that one experience it follows that *"Everything that is good will fall apart after 3 years and I will be abandoned."*

As an established core-negative belief it had played itself out in a three-year pattern all through her life. And the fact was, it would continue to do so until she forgave her parents for abandoning her. That simply is the way it works.

Although, on the face of it, there always seemed to be a logical reason for losing her job, the fact of the matter was that it was never by accident. She had unconsciously 'created' that situation of being abandoned or rejected by her boss, or the company, so it would fit her story. This is a good example of the principle that states that we tend to create reality through our thoughts and beliefs.

But there was purpose in it beyond her need to be right. Her own Spiritual Intelligence had engineered each experience in order to bring the unhealed abandonment by her parents to the surface, so it could be healed. To that end, she had actually *enrolled* the people in the company to fire her.

She was not aware of it, of course, and neither were those who fired her. There would have seemed good reason for it on every occasion, even situations that arose that had nothing to do with her personally, like the firm going bust or moving.

But the fact remains that she created an energy field that organized the energy of the company in such a way as to create circumstances in which she would be out of a job, feeling abandoned and rejected. What she needed to do was to see the pattern and recognize the opportunity. That's exactly what she had done and was the reason why she was at the workshop.

Childhood traumas are nearly always unresolved and remain repressed. Children don't have the emotional maturity to work through a major emotional event like someone dying, a parent leaving, or parents being violent and so on. So the rule is that anything repressed in childhood is likely to be played out in adulthood as a way for it to become resolved.

Last night I was watching the Tavis Smiley show on PBS. He was interviewing Mickey Rourke, the nominee for best actor in the Academy Awards for his brilliant performance in the movie, The Wrestler. He gave one of the most honest and authentic interviews I have ever seen. Even Smiley said that few interviewees have been so candid, open and vulnerable on the show in the all the years he had been doing them than this man.

They were exploring the parallels between the film and his own life, and Rourke told how he had risen high in the acting profession and then, as he put it, "All my issues and inner demons started to get a hold of me and I totally sabotaged myself." He became so difficult and obnoxious that no one would cast him in any film. He crashed.

Mickey described how he'd learned, early on, to cover his insecurities and wounds by being tough, hard and ruthless.  He said he had armored his body with muscle as a form of protection and kept his heart totally closed.  His way of being with people was to dominate them.

One day he looked in the mirror and saw what he had become.  He realized that the facade of strength was, in fact, his greatest weakness and it had ruined him.  One can only hide behind an alter-ego for so long.

The real Mickey Rourke was a frightened, hurt and extremely insecure person — still a child really.  He realized that the only way he could regain his emotional health and claw his way back to being an actor, was to confront his demons as he called them and become real.  He needed to become vulnerable and accountable.  He went back to his favorite sport, boxing.

That helped him channel his anger and work it through, but it also taught him to focus and be committed to what he was doing.  He took on small insignificant parts in questionable movies just to get back in and rebuild his image.  He was totally responsible, committed and accountable.  Over a period of 13 years, he slowly built up his reputation again and finally landed the part in The Wrestler.

He shared with Smiley that throughout all those years he was seeing a spiritual counselor of some sort.  He didn't say what kind, except to stress it wasn't a psychotherapist.  Neither did he elaborate, but it was clear that this person was a tremendous support to him and remains so today.  I assume he or she, over the years, helped him confront his demons and work them through.  Mickey did not say what they were, but we can imagine.  And I would bet that the need to forgive his parents was high on the list.

Right at the end of the interview, Tavis Smiley tentatively asked a question that went something like this. "Mickey, when you look at the whole story of your life and how everything came together, all the right people showing up right when you needed them, even the crash itself, is there a part of you that wonders whether it was all Divine intervention?"

Rourke didn't hesitate. "Absolutely." he said. I have no doubt whatsoever. It was God's plan for me." He was hinting at what is at the core of the Radical Forgiveness philosophy — God does not make mistakes.

This kind of thing does not happen to just a few people. It happens to everyone. It is all part of the human journey, and it provides us with our spiritual lessons. But it helps to be able to recognize when this is occurring. In the essay with which I end this book, entitled *Healing at Work* [see page 121], I show how this drive to heal toxic beliefs and old childhood wounds can cause people to exhibit problematic behavior at work and can cause havoc within the organization, not to mention creating great damage to their careers.

The story is fictional, but it is, nevertheless, a cautionary tale that every executive, business manager and business owner should heed as a matter of survival. It is a dramatic illustration of how our unconscious hidden agendas can literally bring a company to its knees — without anyone involved understanding how or why it happened. Understanding the healing mechanism and providing the means for it to occur without it upsetting the applecart amounts to wise management of human capital.

15

In my book, *Spiritual Intelligence at Work,* I cite the example of a mid-level executive named Dave, whose father was one of those men who seemed to delight in putting their sons down and making them feel inadequate. He was always telling young Dave, *"You'll never be any good. Look at you. Your brother will go a long way in life, but not you. You don't have what it takes to be anything at all other than something mediocre at best."*

That was a terrible wound, and it went deep. It also became a toxic, core-negative belief that he carried in his subconscious mind all through his life. It showed up in his life many times but the big reaction came when he was promoted from being a mid-level executive (in his mind a mediocre position), to a senior executive.

Being a senior executive did not fit his story that he would never be more than mediocre, so what did he do? He began to sabotage himself and all those who worked for him in order to initiate failure. He made bad decisions, and created problems everywhere. He treated his workers badly, unconsciously doing to them what his father had done to him, putting them down and humiliating them. He created a lot of conflict within his department and began to find reasons to resist the authority of his own boss, reacting to him like he was his father. His boss reacted angrily and threatened to fire him if he didn't shape up.

Fortunately, with some assistance from his coach, a person trained in handling work-related Radical Forgiveness situations, he suddenly recognized what was happening. He realized that he was acting out some original pain and that, whatever it was, it had come to the surface for healing. The big clue was in seeing how he was projecting all his rage onto his boss with whom he'd had a good relationship prior to the promotion. It suddenly became obvious to him that his boss represented his father. At that point he knew he had to forgive his father if he was to avoid creating a disaster for himself and those who worked for him.

He enrolled in the *Online 21 Day Program for Forgiving Your Parent(s)* [see page 207], and forgave his father. That literally saved his career.

This example shows very clearly why we need to forgive our parents for whatever they did or said to us that wounded us. It can be a matter of survival. It also demonstrates how our Spiritual Intelligence will attract into our experience people who will provide opportunities to heal our pain by either, as in this case, representing the person who caused our pain in the first place, or mirroring back to us our own self-hatred. David might have been beastly to his subordinates because he could see in them his own powerlessness, impotence and fear he experienced when his father would rail at him.

I could give hundreds of examples of stories that show why we need to forgive our parents for what they did to us, or what we think they did to us. What determines whether people have good, healthy relationships, or a string of disastrous, five year long liaisons that ought never to last longer than five minutes, is whether or not they forgive their parents for the very things that get acted out in these dysfunctional relationships.

It is paradoxical that the only thing that keeps us in such seemingly toxic relationships is the need to heal our pain.

17

Much better that we realize this fact and do something proactive about it like forgiving our parents. If only we would realize that most of the difficulties that arise even in the best of relationships have their origins in the emotional baggage that we each bring to the relationship and that every upset is an opportunity to heal it, life would be much easier.

It seems clear to me that most, if not all, addictions have their origins in the wounds of childhood. Whatever the substance of choice, whether it be alcohol, drugs, food, work or sex, the purpose of its use is to medicate the pain of the addict's childhood. Most of them never get free from it. Even in the 12 step programs — which I feel are divinely inspired — few people get beyond Step Four. This step requires them to take a moral inventory of themselves and confront their demons. Rather than face them, they stop there and, as dry drunks, become addicted to meetings instead.

I was having dinner with a friend of mine in a restaurant in Houston, Texas. We had just completed a weekend workshop. A friend of Karen's stopped by our table and we invited him to join us. He was very involved in AA and had been sober 14 years. He explained how he was able to give up his addiction after discovering that the pain he was medicating was that his mother had sexually abused him from age four to ten, or thereabouts. Then he said this. "But you know, Karen, I will never be free of my addiction until I know why she did that."

Up until this moment, I had been quiet during this whole conversation, but at that point I piped up, "Then you're screwed, aren't you!" He looked at me with an expression that indicated that he thought I was some kind of screwball, daring to challenge what he thought was wisdom garnered from years of contemplating his suffering. "What do you mean by that?" he asked.

"I mean that you are making your becoming free of your addiction dependent on a totally unanswerable question," I replied. "Your mother did not know why she did that to you. You will never know why she did it to you. No one will ever know why she did that to you. That's a victim's question and it will keep you enslaved to your addiction for the rest of your life."

He did not like it. "So what would you suggest, then?" he demanded to know with a derisory look on his face that suggested an expectation that I would have no adequate answer.

"Hang out in a different question," was my immediate answer.

"What would that be? he snapped back.

"Instead of asking why she did it," I answered, quietly. "How about asking yourself; I wonder what the gift might be in her having done that to me that I might not, at this moment, be seeing? It's an equally unanswerable question but a much more empowering question to hang out in. It removes you from being a victim, which is what you have been all your life, even during your 14 years of sobriety." He said little to me after that and I let it drop.

The next day, he called me. "I have been awake all night thinking about what you said, and I want to thank you.

You have saved my life. I am now totally free for the first time. I don't know what the actual gift is or was, but it doesn't matter. I got the message."

The point of this story is that it highlights the difference between traditional forgiveness and Radical Forgiveness. If I had said to him, "Yes, your mother was a very bad mother and an abuser, but in order to be free you need to forgive her," nothing would have changed. He would probably have protested that he had already forgiven her and very likely he had done so in traditional forgiveness terms — and only to the extent that traditional forgiveness is likely to be effective, which is hardly at all.

If he hadn't already forgiven her and had asked my advice about how to forgive her, I would have been unable to give any practical advice since there is no methodology for that kind of forgiveness. Those that advocate it can only say that you must make the decision to let go; release the need to blame; release the anger, let bygones be bygones, etc. But these are just platitudes. The question that always remains is HOW?

No matter how hard you try to let bygones be bygones, the fact is that for as long as you continue to consider yourself victimized, forgiveness will forever elude you. The need to condemn nearly always overrides the desire to forgive, no matter how hard we try. That's why forgiveness is universally considered being a very difficult thing to achieve.

It is a measure of how rare it is that someone who does somehow manage to forgive a person for committing a heinous crime against them, gets to be interviewed by

Oprah on national television. It makes for good ratings because all those watching know full well that they couldn't do it, and by implying that only very special and extraordinary people can achieve forgiveness, they can rest comfortably in that knowledge about themselves and feel okay about continuing to blame and seek retribution.

What I did with this AA person was to give him an opportunity to reframe his story in a way that suggested that there was some meaning and purpose in what his mother did, and that what he perceived was done TO him was actually done FOR him. This is the Radical Forgiveness concept and, as you can see, it is radically different from traditional forgiveness.

The assumption here (and all that I am proposing here is only an assumption), is that at some level his own soul had asked to have the experience of being sexually abused as part of his reason for being on the earth plane at this time. As it is with all of us, the purpose for being here is to learn and grow spiritually, and most of what we experience on this earth plane while we are here is pre-planned, purposeful and Divinely guided. Being willing to be open to this possibility is all that is required in doing Radical Forgiveness. There is no requirement that you believe it.

It is highly likely that his soul and that of his mother had decided in advance of their incarnation to create the circumstances of his childhood so that he would become an addict and then, as he graduated from that experience, fulfill his mission to help other souls move through their lessons.

# The Soul's Journey Through Life

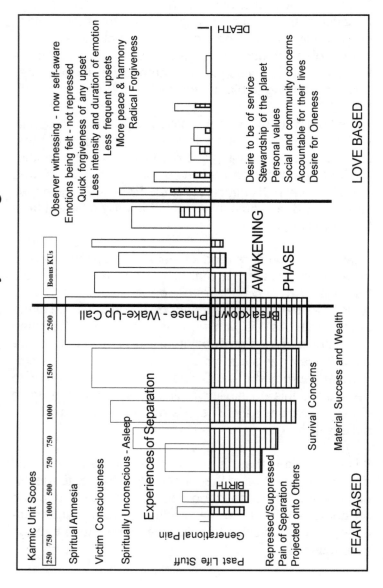

This man was clearly doing this, for he had sponsored many hundreds of people over the years and helped them do likewise upon their healing. I feel that people like him who choose the path of addiction, especially alcoholism, are the ones who have opted to take on the maximum amount of spiritual growth that any soul could endure in a single lifetime, and that their contribution to the spiritual evolution of the collective consciousness can hardly be imagined.

If this is true, it brings us to the inescapable conclusion that we choose our parents, and we do so with great care. Having decided how much spiritual growth we want to have in this lifetime, we choose parents who will provide the foundation for the learning that will occur in the first part of our life before we begin the process of Awakening. This whole idea is explored at depth in my book, *Getting to Heaven on a Harley,* but basically the idea is as follows:

> As spiritual beings we are always in the process of evolving. At some point in our evolution we are required to expand our sense of what Oneness really means. As Marshall McLuhan once said, "The last one to discover water is likely to be the fish." So it is with oneness. Until we have experienced the opposite of it, it is difficult to appreciate its nature.

> That being the case, we ask to have the high privilege of incarnating into a world characterized by physical duality and separation in order to gain that awareness. To the extent that we experience separation in our lifetime, so do we magnify our appreciation of the truth of oneness.

It is a very important lesson for us to learn and it is no easy assignment, especially since, for much of our incarnation experience we have little or no memory of the spiritual world and our having been part of it. Spiritual amnesia is essential, at least for the first phase of the journey; otherwise we wouldn't play the game of life. We would all know that it was a setup and, therefore, would never get to feel the pain of separation essential for our spiritual growth.

We also agreed to be willing to experience separation as an emotional event. For that a body was essential. Since the definition of an emotion is 'a thought attached to a feeling,' it was obvious that mental awareness would not be enough.

Without a body to provide the feeling element, you would have only the thought form. Hence, the primary purpose of bringing our vibration low enough to form a physical body is to give us the opportunity to feel the feelings connected to the thought form, *"I am separate."* Only then can we experience it emotionally. The human experience is meant to be an emotional one, and to the extent that we don't allow ourselves to have our emotions is the degree to which we are denying our purpose for being here.

Having a body, then, gives us the opportunity not only to (falsely) experience ourselves as separate from each other in the physical sense but to experience the pain of separation emotionally. This is achieved through a variety of mechanisms such as betrayal, abandonment, rejection, withholding of love, criticism, judgment, control, divorce, abuse, neglect, discrimination, imprisonment, poverty, racialism, ethnic cleansing, genocide, rape and so on. When you look around the world and at your own lives currently, you can see that life on planet Earth provides plenty of opportunity for everyone to experience separation. Some choose one form of separation while other choose something else.

But the fact is we are all experiencing separation in one way or another, and we are all giving others the opportunity to feel it; albeit in a very diverse fashion depending on circumstances. It's all part of the Divine plan.

Each soul agrees to experience a certain amount of separation (represented as 'karmic units' in the diagram below), before beginning their Awakening phase. Once that goal has been reached, the Ego, which is your guide for the first phase, hands you on to your Higher Self, your guide for the Awakening phase and beyond.

This usually occurs around the half-way point in your life; around 50 - 60, very often after a breakdown of some sort. Your Higher Self, or your Spiritual Intelligence if you prefer that term, guides you towards specific books, workshops, programs and particular people that prompt you to begin remembering who you are. All of a sudden you begin to see things differently and become aware of synchronicities and subtle guidance coming from within. Life takes on a whole new meaning and things like Radical Forgiveness seem to make perfect sense to you now, where before you would have said it was crazy.

What this means is that, since the whole thing is Divinely guided, nothing wrong is happening. Each soul is living out its intention to grow and evolve and to help every other soul it comes in contact with to do the same.

Coming back now to parents and why we need to forgive them, it begins to be obvious that (a) we chose them and they agreed to be our parents; (b) that in how they raised us, no matter whether it was with love and devotion or with neglect and abuse, they were doing exactly what we wanted them to do; and (c) what they did to hurt or damage us was essential to our spiritual growth and it was what we signed up for.

Think about it. Who better than our own parents to provide, during our most vulnerable years, the earliest experiences of separation — ones we would likely repeat many times over for 40 years or more, prior to our Awakening, as a way to leverage those early experiences?

By and large, they taught us everything we know about ourselves by what they said, or didn't say — to us or about us; what they did or didn't do — to us and for us; and by how they reacted to us whenever we ventured to express our true nature. Some of what they shamed us with became the shadow material that would later fuel opportunities to experience the pain of separation, both within ourselves and with others.

It is a role that falls naturally upon parents. They have no choice in the matter. *(If you are a parent, you know this for yourself. It is simply thrust upon you.)* Neither do parents have training in or even, in many cases, an awareness of that awesome responsibility that begins to weigh heavily even before the birth. They can do no better than stumble along, doing the best they can with little knowledge, scant experience and the most meager set of tools to assist them in nurturing an emerging human being. If parents were perfect, we would be denied the opportunity to learn and grow through the pain of separation which is the whole point of being here.

We must remember too, that just like everyone else, most parents are wounded human beings themselves and, like everyone else, have a tendency to project their pain onto others, most often onto those they love, particularly those they can influence the most and over whom they have power and control — their children. They also have no choice but to pass on their own values and morals, codes of behavior, skills, attitudes, prejudices, dreams, thought habits and so on to their children. It is impossible for them not to do that.

Research shows that even in what we might judge as 'nice' homes, children grow up hearing about 20 negative messages about themselves for every one positive message. Taking all this into account, it is hardly surprising that most of us inferred from the way they carried out this role, that we were somehow not okay, or that we were flawed in some particular way, or that we should not expect to be successful, rich, powerful or deserving.

Add to this the fact that the most frequently used and most damaging form of punishment employed by most parents — especially in middle-class families — is the prolonged withholding of love, and you begin to understand why so many people feel that they are not lovable. Childhood woundings run the gamut from the most ter-

27

rible forms of physical and sexual abuse, to a parent show-ing a very subtle preference for a sibling; from  walking out of a child's life and never contacting him or her again, to making a careless remark or joke that simply hits home. Some of what came to mean so much to a child in his or her later life might have been nothing more than a seem-ingly innocuous remark.

Add to the mix rejection, abandonment, repeated criticism, put-downs, abuse, broken promises, let-downs, perfec-tionism, control etc,. and it becomes obvious just how much potential parents have to create the separation you require for your spiritual growth, and that their perfection lies in their utter imperfection.

This might be a good moment to review your own list of things your parents did that you feel were wounding in some way. As you do this, remember that at the human level, they were doing the best they could and in most instances were totally unaware that they were doing or saying things that might have been wounding to you. Your parents may have been wonderful people but might have hurt you quite unwittingly. I also realize that you may love your parents and have a strong resistance to criticizing them, preferring instead to deny your own pain.

So, the best way to approach this exercise is to treat it like a piece of personal research, detaching it from any blame or recrimination.  This process becomes much easier, too, if you remember to also view it from the spiri-tual perspective; that they did what they did because you asked them to do it for your soul's growth and that no matter what happened, nothing wrong or bad actually occurred.

Check the following complaints and see if you identify with the core-negative belief in italics. If it's different, write it in.

### The I AM NOT-ENOUGH Syndrome.
☐ Demanding impossible perfection from me.
*(I will never be enough.)*
☐ Not being there for me emotionally.
*(I don't matter.)*
☐ Not caring about me.
*(I'm not worthy.)*
☐ Not listening to me.
*(I've nothing good to say.)*
☐ Not giving me approval/acknowledgment/praise.
*(I'm not valued.)*
☐ Not taking much notice of me.
*(I am invisible.)*
☐ Not loving me enough.
*(I'm not lovable.)*
☐ Not touching me enough, or even at all.
*(Something's wrong with me.)*
☐ Always comparing me against my siblings.
*(I don't measure up.)*

### The I AM NOT OK Syndrome
☐ Wanting me to be different from the way I was/am.
*(I'm not OK.)*
☐ Wanting me to be the other gender.
*(I'm a disappointment.)*
☐ Wanting me to be what they needed me to be.
*(I am not OK.)*
☐ Controlling me all the time.
*(I am powerless.)*
☐ Making everyone more important than me.
*(I don't matter.)*
☐ Manipulating me all the time.
*(I have to please everyone.)*

29

☐ Always criticizing me.
> *(I am bad.)*

☐ Always putting me down/making me wrong.
> *(I am wrong.)*

☐ Always blaming me, even when it was not my fault.
> *(It's always my fault.)*

☐ Not allowing me to speak or be seen.
> *(I'm invisible.)*

☐ Not allowing me to express myself truthfully.
> *(I have to be what I'm not to be loved.)*

☐ Not allowing me to express my feelings.
> *(Feelings are not OK.)*

☐ Not allowing me to express my creativity.
> *(I have to play safe.)*

☐ Not allowing me to follow my own career/life purpose.
> *(I have to please them, not me.)*

## The ABANDONMENT SYNDROME

☐ Leaving me.
> *(I am worthless.)*

☐ Dying and others not telling me the truth.
> (It was my fault.)

☐ Mother gave me up for adoption.
> *(I'm expendable; not wanted.)*

☐ They divorced ☐ Mother ☐ Father left.
> *(My feeling don't count.)*

☐ Not wanting me even to be born.
> *(I'm not wanted then or now.)*

☐ Making me look after my younger siblings.
> *(I have to be responsible.)*

☐ Dumping his/her pain on me.
> *(I am responsible for them.)*

☐ Making me responsible for everything.
> *I come second.)*

☐ Taking my childhood away from me.
> *(My life doesn't count.)*

**The ABUSE SYNDROME**

☐ Punishing me all the time for even small transgressions.
*(I am wrong.)*

☐ Giving me punishment out of proportion to the 'crime.'
*(I am unworthy.)*

☐ Beating me severely and often.
*(I am bad.)*

☐ Punishing by withholding love/approval for long periods.
*(Love is a weapon.)*

☐ Shaming me about my sexuality.
*(I am bad - my body is bad.)*

☐ Sexually abusing me.
*(I am powerless and bad.)*

☐ Allowing others to sexually abuse me.
*(I am worthless and can be used.)*

☐ Didn't protect me from sexual abuser
*(I am not heard.)*

The value of doing this lies in the fact that it represents the first stage in the process of Radical Forgiveness, there being five stages in all. These are:

1. Telling the Story
2. Feeling the feelings
3. Collapsing the Story
4. Reframing the Story
5. Integrating the New Story

**1. Telling the Story.** It is very important that we begin the forgiveness process from where we are, which is in a state of un-forgiveness. We feel we have been victimized in some way. It is important that we give voice to that victim story so we can have it validated and witnessed, preferably by another person, but it can be ourselves just as easily. By going through the checklist, I am certain that you were reminded of those times when your

31

parents created pain in you and could easily have written a story about each incident.

**2. Feeling the Feelings.** This usually arises out of the process of telling the story. In fact, the checklist process may well have triggered some emotions in you already. This is the vital step that many people want to leave out thinking that they shouldn't have 'negative' feelings. That misses the crucial point that you cannot heal what you don't feel.

Bear in mind, too, that there is no such thing as a negative feeling. Feelings like fear, anger, or grief are not negative. They are simply normal human emotions we all feel from time to time to varying degrees. Labeling them as negative results in people struggling against them, trying to "think positive," or denying them. This only leads people to suppress, repress and project them onto others, onto their own bodies, or onto situations. Resistance to any of our human emotions creates serious internal stress and ultimately causes disease.

**3. Collapsing the Story.** We are not yet in Radical Forgiveness mode at this step, but it nevertheless helps us to move in that direction when we begin to see how, as young children, we might have constructed our story on a lot of spurious interpretations and made assumptions that simply were not true. Or that we had been holding expectations of ourselves or others that could never be met.

Stripping out all these interpretations and seeing just the facts takes a lot of the energy out of the story. So it does too when we become willing to cut our parents some slack and realize that they had their own problems, wounds and issues to deal with in their own lives. How could we expect them to be perfect?

**4. Reframing the Story.** Steps number one, two and three could easily be used in traditional forgiveness, but it is here, at this fourth step, where the two forms of forgiveness part company. With traditional forgiveness, victim consciousness is still part of the mix because there remains a belief that something bad happened. Not so with Radical Forgiveness. This is the step where we have to abandon our victim consciousness and be willing to see the spiritual perfection in the situation.

The analogy I like to use is that of a tapestry. If we look only at the back of the tapestry, it has very little meaning. It is only when we turn the tapestry around and see the front of it that we see the perfection in it. Our victim story, with all its assumptions we hold about life in general — our current world view — equates to the back of the tapestry. If we were able to see the front of the tapestry we would see beyond the illusion and realize the truth of what is. Our changed world view would mean we would 'frame' everything differently, including our story.

When we do the reframe, we are symbolically turning the tapestry over and seeing the truth — i.e., that in spite of all apparent evidence to the contrary provided by our senses, there is complete perfection in the situation. Nothing wrong ever happened so there is nothing to forgive. God does not make mistakes.

This step asks a lot of us, especially if what our parents did was really bad, but fortunately we only need to be

33

willing to open to this possibility. It is essentially a fake-it-till-you-make-it proposition. It is the tools that Radical Forgiveness provides that make it possible. (See below).

**5. Integrating the New Story**. All our victim stories have their own energy fields and these energy fields remain in our physical body for as long as we hold onto the stories. In that sense we might say that our victim stories live in every cell of our bodies. The purpose of this last step is to clear our bodies of those energy fields and replace them with the energy of the new story. We do this by doing something physical as part of the forgiveness process. This can be as simple as writing something, or dancing it out, or walking across a circle as we do when we do the Radical Forgiveness Ceremony.

**The Radical Forgiveness Tools — Secular Prayer**
I have designed a number of tools that take people through these five stages. When I first created them, way back in the early 90s, I didn't realize that they were anything more than a checklist. It was not clear to me at the time that they would actually create an energetic shift in the person doing it and, even more surprising, in the person being forgiven. I have seen it happen so many times now I know that it does do just that. I now also understand that the act of doing a worksheet, or using one of the other tools in the arsenal, activates our Spiritual Intelligence. This is the part of us that knows how to connect with Universal Intelligence, so in that sense the Radical Forgiveness tools constitute what I now call secular prayer.

Many of the tools are readily available, free of charge to anyone who wants to use them and are to be found on our website, www.radicalforgiveness.com along with many downloads and free reads.

You will find a free Radical Forgiveness online worksheet that you can type your responses into if you wish, or download a hard copy version if you prefer to write it out. I urge you to try it because I am convinced that Radical Forgiveness only works if you use the tools. Our consciousness is not yet ready to fully integrate the basic ideas of Radical Forgiveness. Our intellectual intelligence is not adequate to the task; neither is our emotional intelligence. The only part of us that is able to work with it is our Spiritual Intelligence, and I know of no other way to activate this than through the use of one or more of the tools.

After I had taken Gwen through the first two stages as I described earlier, I took her through a session of Satori Breathwork in order to integrate the shift (Step 5), and to bring her to a realization of the truth in the reframe (Step 4). I spent the next whole day with her and the 14 other people in the workshop going over this worksheet, making sure she had got it. She left the workshop in a state of pure bliss.

For your convenience I include a version of the worksheet here as a way to finish out this chapter, so you at least have a version of it to refer to. I trust it will be helpful. I have not changed it to be specific to your parent(s) so that it will be more or less the same as the ones you download from the website at no charge. I have also included additional instructions for each step which I think will be helpful as a reference when you are using the ones you download.

However, there is a very powerful online program available from the website that is absolutely specific to forgiving your parents. It is called, ***"Breaking Free," A 21-day***

### *Program for Forgiving Your Parents.*

This is a paid program in which I set out, in Part One, the basics of Radical Forgiveness. Then, once you commence Part Two, at a time of your own choosing, I send you a specific task to do each day for 21 days.

My expectation is that you will have completely forgiven your parent by the 21st day and that you will be totally free of the pain. I strongly suggest that you take a look at this program located on our website and decide whether or not this is something you would like to do for yourself. [See Page 207].

We also have an online 21-day program for Forgiving Your Partner. It is a very similar structure to the one for parents, but because our partners often represent our parent of the opposite sex, there is a good argument for doing this one first. [See page 209.]

# The Radical Forgiveness Worksheet
## (With Additional Instructions)

### 1. Telling the Victim Story

*[Questions to ask yourself: What am I upset about? With whom? Why? What did he/she/it/they do to me? Really BE the victim. No spiritual overlays or making excuses. Attach your pre-written story to this but add anything you want to on this page to increase your victimhood.]*

### 2a. Confronting the Person Who Victimized You
"_____ ,I am upset with you because . . . "

*[If the event occurred when you were a child or your victimizer had power over you in some other way, it is probable that you were not able to shout back, retaliate or confront the person. So this is your chance to do so. Tell the person (or organization) how much it has hurt or damaged you. Really BE the victim. No spiritual overlays or excuses. Tell it like it was or is.]*

### 2b. Feeling the Feelings
Because of what you did (are doing), **I FEEL:**

*[Identify your real emotions here. Use feeling words. Sad, angry, betrayed, hurt, rejected, resentful, rageful, vengeful, etc.]*

### *(Now Acknowledging Your Own Humanness)*

**3.** I lovingly recognize and accept my feelings, and judge them no more. I am entitled to my feelings.

| Accept: | Willing: | Skeptical: | Unwilling: |
|---|---|---|---|
| | | | |

**4.** I own my feelings. No one can make me feel anything. My feelings are a reflection of how I see the situation.

| Accept: | Willing: | Skeptical: | Unwilling: |
|---|---|---|---|
| | | | |

*[This is an empowering step because you are taking your power back by owning responsibility for your feelings. When we say others make us feel angry, we give them power over us.]*

37

*[Secondly, your feelings give you a tremendous amount of feed-back about how you perceive the situation — usually as a victim. Knowing that, you are then in a position to choose to see it differently and then alter your feelings about it.]*

### 5. Holding Judgments and Expectations

My discomfort was my signal that I was withholding love from myself and _____ by judging, holding expectations, wanting _____ to change and seeing _____ as less than perfect. *(List the judgments, expectations and behaviors that indicate that you were wanting him/her/them to change.)*

*[When we judge a person (or ourselves) and make them wrong, we withhold love. Even when we make them right, we are withholding love, because we make our love conditional upon their rightness continuing. Any attempt to change some-one involves a withdrawal of love, because wanting them to change implies that they are wrong (need to change) in some way. Furthermore, we may even do harm in encouraging them to change, for though we may act with the best inten-tions, we may interfere with their spiritual lesson, mission, and advancement. It is also revealing to see how many of these judgments and expectations you are making about your-self. You could be looking in the mirror!]*

## *(Now Beginning to Collapse the Story)*

**6.** I now realize that in order to feel the experience more deeply, my soul has encouraged me to create a BIGGER story out of the event or situation than it actually seemed to warrant, considering just the facts. This purpose having been served, I can now release the energy surrounding my story by separating the facts from the inter-pretations I have made up about it.

*[Much of our pain is in our being invested, not so much in the **facts** of what happened, but in what we **made up** about what happened. e.g. Granddad died — he abandoned me. My mother divorced my Dad — she drove my father away from me. My husband cheated on me — I must no longer be sexually attrac-*

38

*tive. I was sexually abused — all men will hurt me. My father was
emotionally unavailable to me — I'll never be enough. So here
you would list the main interpretations and indicate whether the
level of emotion and attachment you have around each interpre-
tation is still, at this moment in time, high, medium, low or at zero.]*

### 7. Core-Negative Beliefs I Either Made Up From My Story or Which Drove the Story. *(Check Those That Apply)*

☐ I will never be enough. ☐ It is not safe to be me. ☐ I am always last or left out. ☐ People always abandon me. ☐ It is not safe to speak out. ☐ I should have been a boy/girl. ☐ No matter how hard I try, it's never enough. ☐ Life's not fair. ☐ It is not good to be powerful/successful/rich/outgoing. ☐ I am unworthy. ☐ I don't deserve. ☐ I must obey or suffer. ☐ Others are more important than me. ☐ I am alone. ☐ No one will love me. ☐ I am unlovable. ☐ No one is there for me. ☐ Other

_____

## *(Now Opening to a Reframe)*

**8.** I now realize that my soul encouraged
me to form these beliefs in order to mag-
nify my sense of separation so I could feel it more deeply for my
spiritual growth. As I now begin to remember the truth of who I am,
I give myself permission to let them go, and I now send love and
gratitude to myself and _____ for creating this
growth experience.

## *(Noticing a Pattern and Seeing Perfection In It)*

**9.** I recognize that my Spiritual Intelligence has created stories in the
past that are similar in circumstance and feeling to this one in order
to magnify the emotional experience of separation that my soul
wanted. I am recognizing some clues in my life that provide evidence that, even though I don't know
why or how, my soul has created this
particular situation, too, in order that I
learn and grow.

| Accept: | Willing: | Skeptical: | Unwilling: |
|---------|----------|------------|------------|
|         |          |            |            |

[Here you would list similar stories and feeling experiences (as

39

in 2b) and note the common elements in them. The kind of evidence to look out for might be as follows:

**i. Repeating Patterns.** This is the most obvious one. Marrying the same kind of person over and over again is an example. Picking life partners who are just like your mother or father is another. Having the same kind of event happening over and over is a clear signal. People doing the same kind of things to you, like letting you down or never listening to you, is another clue that you have an issue to heal in that area.

**ii. Number Patterns.** Not only do we do things repetitively, but often do so in ways that have a numerical significance. We may lose our job every two years, fail in relationships every nine years, always create relationships in threes, get sick at the same age as our parents, find the same number turning up in everything we do, and so on. It is very helpful to construct a time-line like the one like Steve did (see Page 46), except that you might fill in all the dates and note all intervals of time between certain events. You might well find a meaningful timewise correlation in what is happening.

**iii. Body Clues.** Your body is giving you clues all the time. Are you always having problems on one side of your body or in areas that correlate to particular chakras and the issues contained therein, for example? Books by Caroline Myss, Louise Hay and many others will help you find meaning in what is happening to your body and what the healing message is. In our work with cancer patients, for example, the cancer always turned out to be a loving invitation to change or to be willing to feel and heal repressed emotional pain.

**iv. Coincidences and Oddities.** This is a rich field for clues. Anytime anything strikes you as odd or out of character, not quite as you'd expect or way beyond chance probability, you know you are onto something.

Where once we thought things happened by chance and were just coincidences, we are now willing to think that it is

Spirit making things happen synchronistically for our highest good. It is these synchronicities that lie embedded in our stories, and once we see them as such, we become free then to feel the truth in the statement that "my soul has created this situation in order that I learn and grow."

## *(Noticing the Projection and Taking It Back)*

**10.** I now realize that I get upset only when someone resonates in me those parts of me I have disowned, denied, repressed and then projected onto them. I see now the truth in the adage, "If You Spot It, You Got It!" It's me in the mirror!

| Accept: | Willing: | Skeptical: | Unwilling: |
|---|---|---|---|
| | | | |

**11.** (X)_____ is reflecting what I need to love and accept in myself. Thank you _____ for this gift. I am now willing to take back the projection and own it as a part of my shadow. I love and accept this part of me.

| Accept: | Willing: | Skeptical: | Unwilling: |
|---|---|---|---|
| | | | |

**12.** Even though I may not understand it all, I now realize that you and I have both been receiving exactly what we each had subconsciously chosen and were doing a dance with and for each other to bring us to a state of awakened consciousness.

| Accept: | Willing: | Skeptical: | Unwilling: |
|---|---|---|---|
| | | | |

**13.** I now realize that nothing you, _____, have done is either right or wrong. I am able now to release the need to blame you or anyone else. I release the need to be right about this, and I am *WILLING* to see the perfection in the situation just the way it is.

| Accept: | Willing: | Skeptical: | Unwilling: |
|---|---|---|---|
| | | | |

**14.** I am willing to see that, for whatever reason, my mission or *soul contract* included having experiences like this and that you and I may have agreed to do this dance with and for each other in this lifetime. If it is for the highest good for both of us, I now release you and myself from that contract.

| Accept: | Willing: | Skeptical: | Unwilling: |
|---|---|---|---|
|  |  |  |  |

**15.** I release from my consciousness all feelings of *(as in Box # 2b):* _____

## *(Now the Reframe Statement)*

**16.** The story in Box #1 was your Victim Story, based in the old paradigm of reality (victim consciousness). Now attempt a different perception of the same event (a reframe), from your new empowered position, based on the insights you have experienced as you have proceeded through this worksheet.

*(It may simply be a general statement indicating that you just know everything is perfect, or a statement that includes things specific to your situation if, that is, you can actually see what the perfection is. Often you cannot. Be careful not to do a reframe that is based in World of Humanity terms. Note any positive shift in feeling tone.)*

I now realize that . . .

[The reframe is the thing that people have the most trouble with. They often try to give some explanation of it in World of Humanity terms; what they learned from it about their life, or a decision they made, etc. Those are not invalid interpretations of course, and they might come into the category of *gifts*. But they do not indicate a grasp of the spiritual perfection that was the underlying purpose of the situation — which is the reframe we are looking for.

The original situation as in Box #1, the victim story, was framed by all the thoughts, preconceptions and beliefs that you had about it, and for the most part, they are those that naturally arise out of victim consciousness.

The reframe therefore is an invitation to change the experience by changing your perception of it — in other words, changing how you frame it. Instead of referencing it from the victim standpoint, you frame it with the idea that there is Divine perfection in the situation even though you cannot yet see it.

This is often very difficult to accept, but the good thing about it is that it does not require that we see WHY it is perfect, or that we must GET the lesson involved. It is nearly always beyond our ability to comprehend anyway, so it's a waste of time trying to figure it all out.

You are, in effect, *trying on* the new paradigm; of feeling out what it might feel like to adopt the idea of spiritual perfection. In that sense then, Radical Forgiveness is a *fake it till you make it* process.

Even so, it is possible that, as a result of doing the reframe you might begin to see the situation in a completely different light and begin to move into a feeling of gratitude for the person. If not immediately then perhaps at some future time.]

## *(Now the Final Proclamations)*

**17.** I completely forgive myself, _____ and accept myself as a loving, generous and creative being. I release all need to hold onto emotions and ideas of lack and limitation connected to the past. I withdraw my energy from the past and release all barriers against the love and abundance that I know I have in this moment. I create my life and I am empowered to be myself again, to unconditionally love and support myself, just the way I am, in all my power and magnificence.

**18.** I now SURRENDER to the Higher Power I think of as _____ and trust in the knowledge that this situation will continue to unfold perfectly and in accordance with Divine guidance and spiritual law. I acknowledge my Oneness and feel myself totally reconnected with my Source. I am restored to my true nature, which is LOVE, and I now restore love to _____ . I close my eyes in order to feel the LOVE that flows in my life and to feel the joy that comes when the love is felt and expressed.

**19.** A Note of Appreciation and Gratitude to you _____
. Having done this worksheet I now . . . .

_____

_____

_____

. . . I completely forgive you, _____ , for I now realize that you did nothing wrong and everything is in Divine order. I bless you for being willing to play a part in my Awakening — thank you — and honor myself for being willing to play a part in your Awakening. I acknowledge and accept you just the way you are.

**20.** A Note to Myself . . .

_____

_____

_____

I recognize that I am a spiritual being having a spiritual experience in a human body, and I love and support myself in every aspect of my humanness.

**THE END**

# 2: Journey to Awakening

## By Rev. Megan O'Connor

In Loving Memory of
John J. O'Connor and Renato Azuara-Sagahon

"You're spiritually arrogant," my spiritual mentor said as I presented yet another excuse for not accepting her generous offer to begin a personalized coaching program. "Megan, how can you say you know everything about healing your life and the benefits of the internal spiritual work I am asking you to do—and not do the work?" she asked me.

Thinking you know everything about the Infinite Spiritual Intelligence that works for the good of everyone all the time—even if you cannot recognize it, was Gloria Ramirez' definition of spiritual arrogance. Her words stung, but they rung true in my heart. As she spoke to me, her eyes twinkled as if to say, "There is an unimaginable, wonderful life, waiting to come to you if you trust Spirit and the forgiveness process. Do the work, and your life will be transformed in ways you could never imagine."

At that time, Renato, a man whom I loved deeply and wanted to marry, had just ended our relationship. I missed him and felt rejected; I spent a lot of time crying and trying to understand what I had done to cause him to leave. The pain of this failed relationship provided me with the impetus to take Gloria up on her offer.

Little did I know at the time, however, that the end of that relationship would set me on a path of Radical Forgiveness, serve as a catalyst of change in my life, and guide me into a profound relationship with Spirit as well. Embarking on this journey took courage, but it rewarded me in ways I never could have imagined in advance. When I said goodbye to my boyfriend, I said hello to my father and to my true self.

As I look back now, Gloria actually offered me a choice. I could choose to do my part to transform my life, or I could continue to live the same way I had for the last 46 years, which wasn't totally working for me. So, I agreed to begin what I call "my journey to awakening." At the time, the journey felt challenging, but Gloria knew the power of forgiveness and passionately urged me to complete on a deep level the Radical Forgiveness exercises she gave me. She said to me with confidence, "Megan, if you do your part to heal your life, you are going to have a lot of miracles show up."

**Looking at What Happened in My Childhood**

Gloria began my coaching program by explaining to me that most of our adult behavior patterns actually begin from something that happened when we were children. She asked me to search my earliest childhood memories for what Radical Forgiveness calls "the original pain." To help accomplish this, she gave me a simple tool called the "What Happened Form." She felt sure that filling out the form would help me see what experiences had shaped my belief system about myself and men.

I knew that if I committed to embracing the assignment I could create a turning point in my life. So, I set aside a Sunday afternoon, turned the telephone off, got lots of paper ready, and made a cup of soothing tea. Then I pulled out a large box of old childhood pictures to help me get in touch with feelings and memories from the past.

To my amazement, in all my childhood pictures I looked serious and angry instead of playful and lighthearted like most children. Searching through my memories, I recalled that my intense sadness and anger began during my parents divorce process. I also remembered my father, John O'Connor, saying to me on several occasions, "We are getting a divorce, because your mother tricked me into having a second child." His words had stung—I was the second child—and created within me the belief I had done something to cause their break up. I held onto a secret wish to see them together again in a loving way.

Over the years, my older sister, Lisa, and I visited my father regularly on week-ends. Our visits consisted of children's adventures. My father planned something different for us each visit, such as trips to a museum, ice skating lessons or going to our favorite park. At the park, he read a book, and Lisa and I played hop-scotch, chased the squirrels or fed the pigeons peanuts. In the evening, we'd go to a fine restaurant for dinner—my father's favorite part of the day.

During those adventure-filled weekends, I felt carefree; I wished they would last forever. On Sunday evenings my happiness always turned to sadness, though, and often I went home to my mother's house crying, screaming and wondering if I had done something wrong that prevented me from staying with him.

At those times, I needed reassurance from my father that he loved me, but he was introverted by nature and often stoically emotionless. He often said that even as a teenager he felt the desire to live a life of seclusion as a monk or a priest. An undemonstrative man, rarely, if ever, did he show how he felt in word, action or facial expression. This confused me, because I could sense, see and feel his upset even though he said nothing and showed no emotion when I cried.

During the first years of my parents divorce, both my mother and father attempted to be cordial to each other. Despite the smiles and niceties, I could sense the tension and sadness between them. Often my mind screamed, "What is going on here? Why is everyone smiling but sad on the inside at the same time?" It felt much like the proverbial white, invisible elephant standing in the living room of our life. You couldn't miss "it"; "it" was huge, yet no one talked about "it." We all pretended "it" wasn't there, whatever "it" was. My family's non-verbal communication caused me to feel a lot of anxiety. Therefore, at that young age I decided I couldn't trust peoples' words.

As I moved forward with the Radical Forgiveness exercise I'd been given, I realized that Spirit had bigger plans for me than the happy *Ozzie and Harriet* world I had dreamed of as a child. Yes, I deserved to dream of an idyllic life with my mother, father and sister—and to have that life, but instead Spirit had designed my life as a personal training ground to fulfill my life's purpose. And these experiences provided me with what I needed to achieve that goal.

As I looked at the photographs in that box and thought about my childhood, I realized that having a father who did not express himself prompted me to develop and practice on a daily basis the art of sensing peoples' true feelings and intentions without having to listen to their words. He played the role of my spiritual teacher by creating a classroom in which I could practice using my intuitive gifts with him.

I realized that these intuitive abilities now guide me when I feel lost, give wisdom to friends when they experience emotional turmoil and even have helped me intervene at the right moment to save someone's life. Occasionally, I am used by Spirit as a medium to communicate messages to the living from those who have passed-on. Using my gifts to assist people provides me with the most rewarding moments of my life.

Using the 'What Happened Form' gave me a fresh perspective. It allowed me to see the connection between what I felt as a wounded little girl and repeated in my thoughts and words as an adult. In fact, after each romantic relationship ended I asked myself the same questions: "Why doesn't he love me, and what did I do wrong?" These relationships brought up the same unhealed feelings I had with my father as a young girl. As I looked at the pictures and recalled my childhood, I realized that all of my sadness as an adult actually began as a child. Plus, as an adult I was recreating relationships in which to heal the beliefs that had stemmed from those earlier emotions—that I was unlovable and flawed in some essential way.

As Gloria explained to me later, the beauty of having these discoveries comes in the awareness of issues when they arise again. When or if they do, I now can respond as an adult in the present instead of from the past as a wounded child. I admit that it took a lot of courage to look at myself—to pick up those photos and really see myself then as well as who I had become, but the process freed me.

I continued my Radical Forgiveness work and saw how it created multiple subtle benefits in my life. After completing the 'What Happened Form' on multiple occasions to work on relationships and issues from the beginning of my life to the present, I reread the forms out loud to myself. Surprisingly, the old beliefs I had written about did not have power over me any more. They no longer seemed the truth, and I could see them for what they were—just words on a piece of paper.

The coaching sessions and assignments allowed me to find a new perspective, and to begin to blossom from within. I learned that I served as the creator of my life by the quality of my thoughts. If I thought I wasn't loveable, that's what I created, or at least perceived. If I thought I was loveable, then I experienced myself as lovable and created loving relationships around myself.

### Continuing the Process of Looking at the Past

Knowing that my past held the key to my current issues—especially with men, I continued looking back at my childhood and early adulthood. After high school I began to travel all over the world, and my relationship with my father grew even more distant. At 22, I met the man who soon would become my husband. Not long after our wedding, we moved to another state and began our new life. Our marriage lasted 10 years. Although I could have, while married I never choose to return to the town in which my family lived after my parents' divorce.

During that time, the phone conversations my father and I had were short and impersonal. Once, in what seemed like a bold attempt to get close to him, I said, "I love you Dad."

He responded, "I have to finish the laundry."

I hung up the telephone and cried as I realized that speaking to him felt like speaking to a stranger. Acting on an old thought pattern, I wondered, "What have I done wrong to make him not love me?"

When my own marriage ended, I went into therapy for five years. I also spent 12 years intensely involved in self-transformation seminars, studying spiritual principles and becoming ordained as a new thought, inter-faith minister. Although, I was living life fully, I still didn't know how to be happy. Each one of the spiritual and human potential methodologies and practices I took on uniquely enriched my life and brought me to the next phase of healing.

Yet, in spite these personal accomplishments, I possessed a blind spot in my consciousness that prevented me from seeing all aspects at play in my romantic relationships, choices and career decisions. Like the old invisible white elephant of my childhood, I didn't know what "it" was, but knew it existed in my life and "it" effected my ability to feel happiness. I just couldn't see "it."

## Hearing What My Inner Child Had to Say

To go further into the process of Radical Forgiveness, the next step of my coaching program involved allowing my "Inner Child" to feel and say everything that had gone unsaid throughout my life. Although my conscious mind might not have remembered all these words and feelings, my subconscious mind had not forgotten them. Gloria called this step "learning to process and release emotions in a healthy way." It consisted of letting my Inner Child say whatever she felt but had never expressed.

I discovered that this process brought up a lot of angry emotions in me. I beat a pillow with a tennis racket, cried, wrote in a journal, and even screamed uncontrollably to release negative energy from my body. These methods seemed strange and uncomfortable at first, especially since somewhere I had learned that being spiritual meant being nice all the time.

Over the course of my life this created a pressure-cooker effect; often I exploded when too much pressure built up from my suppressed emotions. I had to go through a slow process to learn how to give myself permission to express my feelings and speak my truth in the moment. The expression "what you resist persists" and "feelings buried alive never die" certainly appeared true for me. For 46 years I had settled for peace (not speaking my truth) at the cost of hiding my true self and my feelings. However, those feelings had not disappeared during that period. They had lived as strongly and fully within me as they had when I first felt them.

I saw the benefits of this self-expression exercise soon afterwards. I had increased energy and the urge to be creative, laugh, play, and not take life so seriously. The urge to play was so strong that I found it hard to resist. For example, one day I stood under an awning at a gas station watching the rain pour down. My free-spirited child within remembered how much joy she felt playing in puddles on a hot summer day. I hesitated for a moment, considering what other people—like my friend sitting in the car—would think of me if I jumped in a nearby puddle. I knew this was one of life's precious moments that I didn't want to miss, so into the rain and the puddle I went jumping and laughing in complete abandonment. Between splashes and laughter, I glanced over at my friend and found she, too, was laughing hysterically.

## Writing Letters of Forgiveness

My next assignment involved writing three forgiveness letters. Gloria told me to write these letters to anyone whom I felt had wronged me. My list inlcuded my father, stepfather, husband, and old boyfriends. I included Renato in the last group. My relationship with Renato felt the freshest, and, therefore, like the one I needed to forgive most; the break up had happened so recently. However, I knew that my relationship with my father had had the most impact on me during the course of my life.

Renato was naturally open hearted, honest and willing to share himself intimately. With a big smile on his face often he would ask me, "Who are you, and who am I to you?" He was curious about people and asked a lot of intriguing, yet funny, questions to get to know you. I found this trait especially endearing since I never experienced this type of closeness with my father.

We both traveled for work, but we spoke on the telephone daily and were good friends. He possessed a natural ability to connect with me on a spiritual level and to sense my emotions; he always knew what I was feeling.

We came from different cultures—he was Mexican and I was American, but we both enjoyed spending our time together enjoying life and loving each other fully, moment to moment. Together we often explored beaches, looked for shells, sat under the stars, cooked for each other, talked about God, and admired the eagles and hawks that lived in our area. Because we were so close, I found it particularly difficult when he called one day and said he wanted to end the relationship. He justified this decision by saying our cultural differences eventually would make our relationship too hard. Once again I felt hurt, angry and wondered what I had done wrong to cause a man not to love me any longer.

The idea of forgiving men, primarily my father and Renato, seemed unfair and daunting. Renato and I had spoken about getting married and having children, but instead he ended the relationship abruptly. Poof! Just like that he was out of my life. My father and I had barely spoken to each other for over five years. I knew my father had been depressed for years; he kept to himself and rarely joined in conversations at family gatherings. This didn't seem to matter to my ego, which questioned why I had to be the one—again—to make the effort to reach out to this man who still appeared unavailable to me. He hadn't even called me on my birthday for a number of years.

Why should I forgive them? My ego resisted this new idea—forgiveness of those who had I felt had hurt me.

On the other hand, I reasoned, not forgiving them meant condemning myself to expanding the life of my "relationship blind spot," which I still could not see into. I knew the information I needed to improve my relationships was hidden there, but I still could not get out of my own mental box to expand my perception to that point. I had one option: surrender and trust Spirit.

I decided to try the letter writing process despite my ego's resistance. I would write letters to my father and to Renato. "Letter one," Gloria explained, "is your time to express all your nasty feelings about your father and Renato. Give them 'the uglies.' Let it rip. Don't hold back in any way."

"What are 'the uglies'?" I asked.

"The uglies are your ugly feelings of rage, hate, sorrow, and hurt," said Gloria. "Let it rip on paper, but you cannot give this letter to them," she explained.

As I wrote the first letter individually to each one of these men, a feeling of righteous anger emerged within me. I did not like feeling this way, and it left me exhausted. Gloria explained that allowing myself to express these emotions caused my consciousness and the energy in my body to shift. "Just embrace and honor your feelings, you have a right to feel your feelings," she advised.

During the course of writing letter two, I had to ask myself if I had ever acted with similar behavior patterns to those exhibited by my father or Renato. I had to answer some tough questions about myself very honestly: Had I ever hurt someone by not communicating with them? Had I ever ended a relationship abruptly with someone who loved me? Was I ever emotionally unavailable or withdrawn from people? Was I unaware of how my behavior hurt others? Sheepishly and reluctantly I reflected on these questions with full intentionality to see the truth about myself. The answers came to me quite clearly.

All of my life I had pointed the finger at men as the cause of my unhappiness, which justified my belief that I was a victim of circumstances. In truth, I was a master at being unavailable, uncommunicative and careless with the people who loved me. I had to feel compassion for myself as I saw that I was the only person responsible for the hurt I had carried around all of my life. Everywhere I had gone until that moment, I had been projecting—not only with my thoughts but also with my actions—these facts: "I'm not lovable, I'm a victim, and I have done something wrong to deserve not being loved."

The Radical Forgiveness process I had undertaken placed new perceptions in front of me that prior to that point seemingly had been hidden in plain sight. Finally, I could see into my relationship blind spot. It became clear to me that Spirit had orchestrated a multitude of details throughout my life to bring me to this point, so I could see the similarities between Renato and my father. On the one hand, Renato served as a reflection of my father, whom I longed to know and with whom I wanted to have a close relationship. On the other hand, both were brilliant men who struggled to express and use their gifts, talents, emotions, and creativity. It seemed as if they both "left me"—Renato by ending the relationship and later leaving the county and my father by divorcing my mother and moving out of our house.

I realized I had often thought, "If only my father would change," or "If only Renato would change his life, then we could be together and be happy." Unconsciously, I lived from the belief that if I could help them change I would be worthy of their love. Once *they* changed, then *my* inherent imperfection would be corrected, and we could live happily ever after. A well-known author Don Miguel Ruiz explains it this way in his works *The Voice of Knowledge*:

> *"We are born in truth, but we grow up believing in lies. One of the biggest lies in the story of humanity is the lie of our imperfection. The only way to end our emotional suffering and restore our joy in living is to stop believing in lies – mainly about ourselves".*

I made these realizations while writing the second letter, and a profound gratitude welled up inside of me for all the men with whom I had been in relationship throughout my life. They no longer looked insensitive and careless but like spiritual friends who showed up to teach me to love myself and to know Spirit. In particular, I found myself feeling grateful to Renato.

The lesson I learned during my Radical Forgiveness process and life coaching program only revealed itself because Renato ended our relationship suddenly, and I found myself at a loss about how to get beyond my pain. It might sound strange to say I now feel grateful he broke off our relationship, but I am.

When I look at the end of my relationship with Renato using human eyes, I feel hurt, angry and rejected since my focus remains on "what he did to me." If I view it through my "Spirit Spectacles," I see that Renato came into my life to reflect to me the unhealed beliefs I held about my father and myself. On a soul level, Renato sacrificed himself, so I might finally heal those issues and know the truth. In other-words, he didn't do anything *to me*; his soul actually worked with Spirit for my highest good. If at that moment I had chosen to close my eyes to the opportunity for healing and continued to be a victim, I would have missed the lessons he came to teach me.

My third letter to Renato read as follows:

*Thank you for being in my life and assisting in my healing. You gave me the experience of a truly loving relationship and taught me that life is precious. Seeing the higher meaning of our relationship and your purpose in my life has made me confident in Spirit, and has allowed me to know that healing always happens if you trust God. You taught me to embrace my power and greatness, to speak my truth in all situations and to have patience and compassion for people's actions. You have been my biggest teacher on many levels, and I am eternally grateful to you.*

*If in the past I said or wrote anything that may have hurt you, I sincerely ask you to forgive me, as I was spiritually asleep and in pain at the time. I forgive and release you freely into the arms of Spirit, and I pray always for your healing and happiness, Renato. I love you unconditionally, and I always will feel grateful to you for your presence in my life.*

Before practicing Radical Forgiveness, I never would have written that letter to Renato.

Later, as my third letter to my father took shape, the fullness of his contribution to my Soul's development appeared as well. It read:

*Growing up in the silence, when we did not talk on a deep inner level, I developed a finely tuned intuition. I needed to learn to use this intuition to fulfill my purpose in life, which manifests in my work as an intuitive spiritual coach. When you did not express your feelings, you showed me that many deep emotions go unsaid while people quietly suffer through them. In particular, parents don't share these feelings with their children, because they don't know how or they want to shield them from pain. I also learned that you can not know the whole inner life of another person and, therefore, the motivation behind their actions. Within every person lies a well of love, even if it is not expressed externally. You taught me to be non-judgmental and discerning while sparking within me a passion for knowing Spirit.*

*I forgive you and I love you unconditionally, and most of all dad, I am proud of who you are.*

Today, I highly value the gifts my father gave me, and in this brighter light he no longer looks like a distant stranger, but, rather, like one of the most committed spiritual teachers I've known. Through my Spiritual Spectacles I see how his soul spent a lifetime of selflessness, silently guiding me to be sensitive to the inner world of people who yearn for unconditional love. Today, when I meet people who are seemingly unavailable, I don't take it personally; instead, I see them as an opportunity to extend unconditional love. He exhibited the qualities of a teacher or a minister and taught them to me, and of that I am proud.

## The Results of Radical Forgiveness Work

Shortly after completing the last letter to him, out of the blue (or out of Spirit) my father called me for the first time in five years. I felt shocked that he called and shocked that he sounded upbeat and wanted to share himself as well as to know everything about my life. It made me so happy to hear him speaking positively instead of using the depressed and cynical language he often had in the past. We talked about books, people, life, relationships, and even God. For the next six months we continued to become close, and we both did our best to share all of our lives with each other.

My Spiritual guidance told me something was changing with my father and urged me to see him very soon. My 47th birthday was coming up, so I flew home to Philadelphia to spend a long weekend with him and the rest of my family. For the first time in many years my father came to greet me at the terminal. Surprisingly, he was waiting there with my mother; the two of them together chatting and drinking coffee like two old friends. As I watched them, a huge amount of love welled up inside of me; I realized Spirit had granted my childhood wish to see my parents peacefully together. That picture remains dear to me and is etched in my memory.

That Saturday, my sister, father and I spent the day together adventuring in a quaint old town. We shopped, rummaged in a used bookstore, went to a farmers' market, and ate lunch in a fine restaurant. It was an enjoyable day reminiscent of our childhood weekends. At my birthday celebration the whole family communicated authentically and intimately, laughing and telling stores.

At one point my father talked about an old friend and family members no longer with us. We laughed at his quirky jokes and stories and were amazed at his openness. As he talked about himself, he began to cry openly. He seemed to be asking for forgiveness for the darker side of his personality he had shown us over the years. He looked like a little boy who really wanted our love and approval. We all cried; I could hardly believe it.

That night my father also revealed to me that he, too, had an intuitive ability to sense people's feelings. However, he felt a bit scared of it and didn't understand this extra-sensory perception at all; he asked me to explain it to him. Every misperception between us began to make complete sense, and I felt like my father and I had come full circle. I explained to him that there was nothing to be afraid of, and that our intuition was as natural as the other five senses. He seemed to take comfort in those words.

Those four perfectly orchestrated days were the last time I saw my father John Joseph O'Connor alive. Three weeks later he passed away. I believe he was at peace and complete with his life. Some of his last words to my sister and I were, "I love you, and I'm proud of you."

Because of the work I've done with Radical Forgiveness, I am not saddened by my father's passing, even though I miss him and wish we could have had more time together. My peace with him at the time of his passing contributed to an easier acceptance of his death. I know my father lives in Spirit and a state of unconditional love. We said everything meaningful to each other we had to say— simply, "I love you." We did not need to say, "I forgive you," because forgiveness occurred naturally out of dropping our judgments and replacing them with higher understanding.

In the remains of my father's earthly possessions, my sister found a certificate for a ministerial program he had completed in the last year of his life—at the age of 77. Becoming a minister represented his life long dream, which he put off from the age of 16. It gave me so much joy to know my father had begun his journey to follow his heart and express himself to a higher degree while at the same time I, too, was embarking on my own journey to awareness and forgiveness—and to become a reverend as well. I take comfort in knowing that we actually had so much in common and that my relationship with him has brought me to this place in my life.

**How Radical Forgiveness Works**

I have learned that relationships are deeper than they appear. No matter what we perceive, we are connected spiritually, our souls dancing together as one. All else constitutes perceptions held in mind that evaporate when brought into greater awareness. It occurred to me that *doing* the forgiveness processes themselves does not provide the genesis for healing at all. Rather, the act of honest self-reflection, expressing repressed emotions, holding a loving intention to forgive others and yourself, and trusting Spirit propels healing to begin.

As I understand it, Radical Forgiveness is a higher perspective that emerges from an internal surrender to Spirit while being willing. As I surrendered my wounded beliefs, I actually surrendered to love. As I released my father's spirit from my pain and took responsibility for it myself, simultaneously I was released as well. Spirit works to rebalance all relationships back to a state of unconditional love. When this balancing occurs as facilitated by Radical Forgiveness, humanity calls it a miracle. In my experience, a life of miracles is the natural order, especially when you live from grace—which Radical Forgiveness grants.

Curiosity intrigued me to want to understand these principles in more depth, so I researched the meaning of forgiveness. The Latin word for forgiveness is *venia*, the root of which is *ven,* as in vain or artery, meaning "to carry life blood towards." It is provocatively the root of the word "Venus," which is synonymous with "love." In ancient Greek, the word for forgiveness is *synchoro*, as in synchronicity. Most reference materials define forgiveness as "granting pardon, love, atonement, allowing another person their weaknesses, and purification of the heart, Soul or sins." The original meaning of sin was the belief in separation from God. It also comes from an archery term in Hebrew that means to "miss the mark."

As I searched for understanding, it all seemed so paradoxical. Again, the truth was hidden in plain sight waiting for me to discover it. For thousands of years, man has known that to hold judgmental and unforgiving thoughts constitutes an act of separation, or sin, from that which created us—God or God's unconditional love. Radical Forgiveness works like a vein that rushes the life force back to us instantly and clears a way for miracles to occur through synchronicity. When we grant pardon, we atone for our misconceptions of ourselves and others. This cleanses the heart and realigns reality, making a pathway for unconditional love to flourish in relationships. Or as Sikhism says, "Where there is forgiveness, there is God Himself."

I concede that Gloria was correct. Indeed, wonderful things have come into my life once I learned to trust Spirit and the forgiveness process. I learned to be happy, and I received more than I could ever imagine in both my relationships and in my life from practicing Radical Forgiveness. I now know my whole life was orchestrated to bring me to this place of self acceptance.

# 3: Forgiving My Beautiful, Wonderful, Crazy Mother

## By Ana Holub

"Forgiveness is my function as the light of the world."

— A Course in Miracles

Sometimes when I see friends with vibrant, healthy mothers, I marvel. One friend told me she thinks of her mother as her best friend. I wonder, "What would it have been like to have had a mother who survived, who taught me the best ways to travel through life, who was sane and clear and able to support me?"

Yes, I marvel and wonder, and I can feel sad and left out, but then I remember I have a choice about how I feel. I remind myself that when my biological mother couldn't give me what I needed, the Divine Mother offered her eternal support. Through my connection to my Divine Mother, I realize I have all the things I longed for in my childhood: a listening ear, an enthusiastic cheerleader, and a kind and knowledgeable guide. Thankfully, I was able to reach this understanding through Radical Forgiveness and *A Course in Miracles*, which gave me the peace and sanity I have today. Growing up in my family wasn't easy; in fact it felt pretty awful at times, but out of that turbulence came a powerful healing.

## My Family Secret

I grew up in suburban New Jersey in the '60s and '70s with upwardly mobile, culturally Jewish parents who focused on education and success. My two sisters and I had our work cut out for us — we needed to conform and succeed. And while we were at it, we tried not to be too miserable. Our family shared good times, and the kids were physically well taken care of. Yet overall, our house vibrated with conflict and deception. We struggled to be a perfect suburban family, and we deceived ourselves and everyone else in the process.

Until my mother's death in 1985, she was a loving, creative, talented, and beautiful woman as well as an accomplished pianist with a wonderful, artistic flair. She also was fearful, confused, confusing, giddy, depressed, silent, unstable, and massively inconsistent. Today a doctor would diagnose her with bi-polar disorder or manic-depressive disorder. As her child, I only knew I loved my mother, but sensed something in our house was deeply and mysteriously wrong.

The split in my mother's mind was extreme and dangerous to her health. My entire family suffered along with her as we swung dizzily from love to anger, confidence to fear and exuberance to panic. While her mood changes were fairly obvious, most of our swinging was done silently, almost entirely on interior, psychological levels, because we were all trying so hard to be a "normal, happy family."

We had a secret: Mother was crazy. We also had a bigger, unconscious secret: The whole family was crazy, but we were in deep denial. That dynamic was enough to make all of us run in five different directions, alone, confused and without any help or spiritual guidance.

Living at my house felt surreal at times. As a child, I had the hardest time with "Double Mom." One Mom was real— the loving, caring, tender one. The other Mom was erratic, occasionally aggressive, often withdrawn, and definitely not to be trusted. I never knew which one would appear at any moment, which scared me and gave me nightmares. It seemed as if there were two people living inside my mother. One was kind and wonderful. The other was a group of malevolent phantoms who tortured me and my family. In my reveries, they would unzip my mother, take her out of her body, and replace her with their coldhearted presence. Then they'd zip her back up again, and no one could see the difference. Yet even as a little child, I could tell in an instant who was in residence inside of Mom. I always wondered where she went when the imposters usurped her body, but I didn't know who to ask.

By the time I was 10 or 11, I learned to sense from the smell of the molecules in my house whether this was a "high day" or a "low day." I'd walk in the door and literally sniff the air when I came home from school. When I was in high school, I realized that Mom's manic days could be worse than the despondent ones. My mother in a giddy mood seemed even more exasperating to me than when she felt depressed; she exhibited fewer inhibitions when she was "high," so I never knew what she'd do next. No matter which mood Mom was in, I just wanted to run—as fast as possible—and hide.

67

Depending on the day, or the hour, my mother could drastically change her ideas about life. For instance, one day she'd say, "You need a new winter coat. Let's go buy you a really nice, warm, fancy coat." On another day, however, I'd hear an indignant tirade from her about my "frivolous" behavior when I bought a slightly expensive shampoo. "Frivolous" constituted one of her favorite words on the days when she didn't visit the mall on a manic buying spree.

To cope with the constantly changing vicissitudes at home, I worked hard to become "good." I thought being a good girl would bring me safety and acceptance. I got good grades, sang in the choir and came home on time. Later, when this didn't seem to bring me any success, I tried rebellion and teen angst. I broke the rules, snuck around at night and sampled a variety of drugs for entertainment and self-medication. Though I tried to change "me" by changing my self-image, nothing could heal my heart or my problems at home.

Whether we wanted or agreed with them or not, my sisters and I had roles in society and in our family. My older sister played the part of the "smart one" and my younger sister the part of the "cute one." People called me the "pretty one," but I wasn't so sure.

"Am I beautiful?" I asked my mother more than once.

"Beautiful enough for all ordinary circumstances," she always replied.

I always wondered where she had gotten that line. I wanted her to say, "Yes, honey, you are beautiful in all ways, inside and out." My whole being wanted her love and approval. As my body changed at puberty, I also needed some guidance about how to handle the attention I got from men, and her comment just seemed to hurt rather than to help me. Like most teenagers, I felt vulnerable and confused about life. I knew, though, she was afraid my outer attractiveness would swell my head. She didn't trust my interior, and I didn't trust hers. We mirrored each other perfectly.

## I am Not My Mother

To top it off, by the time I became a teenager she often said to me, "You understand. Of all my daughters, you are the one who's most like me." In response to that remark, I developed chronic gastro-intestinal distress. My father, a doctor, put me on medication, but after a few months I asked for therapy.

I just needed the therapist to tell me, "You are a different person than your mother. You don't sound like her at all." I felt so relieved when I heard those words.

"Thank God!" I thought to myself, "I am not Her. I am not That."

Even though I loved my mother, she was driving me crazy. Sometimes my skin crawled when she was near me, and I backed away when she wanted a hug. Her neediness overwhelmed me at times. I just didn't know what to do, and no one else seemed to have any answers.

I felt so embarrassed when she'd meet my friends and say something really dotty, or forget their names or stare oddly into space. My friends loved her, because they saw her wonderful side. I loved her, too, but she was so unpredictable. I just wanted a mother on whom I could lean. Instead, she leaned on me. I didn't even know what it would be like to feel the comfort and guidance of a sane, healthy mother.

When it was time for me to attend college, I moved 3,000 miles away to escape her and my father, who was a good, loving man but emotionally distant and absorbed in his work. I was suffocating on the East Coast with its intellectual pretensions, living in their New Jersey house and its hidden, unspoken anguish. I needed to get the hell out.

So I went to college on the wild West Coast. During this time, I rejected my family by joining another, experimental spiritual family. Yet I loved my biological family and felt terrible about myself for doing this. I had no idea where I fit in or who I was. Looking for solace in meditation and a spiritual teacher, I changed everything about myself (or so I thought) by taking a new name, emptying my bank account and dropping out of school. I thought this would allow me to leave behind the discomfort of having a crazy mother. A part of me also felt a deep love for God and wanted a much deeper spiritual communion.

My parents had never fully been there for me even though they had tried. Mom seemed incapable of being an adult, and Dad had his hands full caring for her. No one was left to care for me, so I found a new tribe and a new life. I tried to leave my worries behind in New Jersey, letting the New Age in California guide my way.

At the age of 23, I got pregnant. Even though the thought of becoming a mother scared me, I wanted to keep my baby. I had next to no money, little support from the father of the child and my own father stopped speaking to me when I told him about the pregnancy. My mother, however, came to visit and gave me a maternity dress.

Her visit turned out to be a difficult one because her symptoms had progressed. She acted even more erratically, and I found myself vulnerable to the unpredictable roller coaster of her moods. Despite this, her love truly touched me, and I felt grateful for her trust in me. Excited about the new baby, she did her best to bring some light into my world during this dark time.

Then I got the phone call.

My sister's unsteady voice told me our mother had committed suicide that day in the garage, by breathing the exhaust as she lay under the car. She'd taken some sleeping pills to make sure she got clearly to the other side. As I listened to my sister, everything seemed to slow down and my world appeared unreal, as if I'd entered a dream or been suddenly transported to another planet. I remember looking around the room, not being able to register where I lived, who I was or what I felt. In shock, I hung up the phone and sat down on the couch. It was a long time before I could say a word.

A day later, in a daze, I got on a plane and flew home. All of us felt numb, adrift in the wreckage of Mom's deliberate death, barely able to function. I spoke at her funeral and remembered her beauty and her wonderful spirit. Round with child and devastated by grief, I wore the dress Mom gave me. I thought that blue denim tent dress represented her last gift to me, but I was wrong.

## I Begin the Forgiveness Journey

In addition to being pregnant, at the time of my mother's death I had no partner and no money. I had friendships and my devotion to Spirit, which saved me, but this was a time when I really wanted the kind, sane, guiding spirit of a mother to help me.

I struggled to go on with life when my own mother had told me that creation, living and survival were just not worth the effort. I wondered why she couldn't have stayed to help me with my new mothering. In addition, I found it almost impossible to cope with all the feelings that came up in me, including relief that her craziness, fear and sadness were gone.

I gave birth to my incredible daughter and lavished my love upon her. I focused on life, not death, and tried to put my sadness aside. It took me eight years to open the emotional box into which I'd placed my grief, confusion, anger, and disillusionment. At that time, I was blessed to attend a retreat called the Enlightenment Intensive, which was modeled on the meditation practice done by Zen monks. At the retreat, I let myself crack open, and I felt the tender emotions I'd previously been afraid to feel. I cried and meditated, then cried, yelled and meditated some more. My grief seemed endless, but eventually I felt clearer, more stable and able to touch a bit more joy. From that day on, I began to have hope in the possibility of my own healing.

Maybe you've had the thought, "If I enter into those memories and feelings, I'll drop into a bottomless pit, and I'll never, ever be able to crawl out again. I better not go there."

I'd had that thought, too. I know exactly how it feels to stand at the edge of the pit, peering with dread into the oblivion that seems so dark and scary and mysterious. It took quite a bit of courage to allow myself to let go … and to trust that somehow I'd survive. I needed to fall, and I let myself take the plunge.

Another eight years went by. One day, I walked into a friend's house and spied *Radical Forgiveness: Making Room for the Miracle* perched on her coffee table. Attracted to its quirky title, I asked to borrow it. As I read the book, I discovered Radical Forgiveness as the missing link in my healing and in my work. Within a month, Colin Tipping came to Mount Shasta to offer a workshop, and I eagerly signed up to participate.

At the seminar, it was clear to me that a lot more layers existed for me to peel away before I could taste true freedom from my past. During one section Colin turned up the music and we all yelled what we really felt; I couldn't even open my mouth. In fact, the rest of the group took a break outside while my workshop partner, Colin and I sat together and did the exercise all over again until I could begin bellowing some serious sound. I was already a rebirther (a style of healing breath work), but I found putting my feelings into specific words incredibly difficult. I sincerely wanted to forgive, yet before Radical Forgiveness, I had no map and no specific steps to help me reach the inner peace I craved. At the workshop, I began to open, learn about myself and feel my emotions, all within a context of honesty and healing.

## Discovering Memories and Puzzle Pieces

With Radical Forgiveness, we learn that whatever happens to us is not random, and even the toughest times have treasures buried within them. To find the gifts in my situation, I had to investigate my memories. I also needed to take a deep look at the interpretations and assumptions I'd made about my relationship with Mom. Only then could I separate truth from fiction.

I'd already discovered one memory during psychotherapy. When I was two, my mother raged at me. She was beginning to show signs of deepening psychological illness, and she had a two year old, a baby and an older daughter to raise. She also was grieving the loss of a son who had died a few years before. So, on that day (and maybe on many days), she really lost it. When I found this particular memory as an adult, I saw her standing over my crib, threatening me with a shoe in her upraised hand. Even though I don't think she actually hit me with the shoe, I was terrified.

I also remembered this: One night when I was about 16, my mother came into my bedroom. She was crying and seemed even more miserable than usual. She apologized for the attack she had made upon me 14 years earlier. At the time, I didn't think it had affected me. After all, I didn't even remember the incident.

"Don't worry about it, Mom," I told her. "It's over."

Years later, however, after I learned about the power of Radical Forgiveness, I noticed how many of my anxieties and insecurities were connected to my life as a toddler. I found they linked intimately with my emerging "victim story," or belief about the world, which often controlled me from the deep lake of my subconscious mind. My victim story said: "I must have done something horribly wrong and, therefore, I must be punished. No one loves me or will take care of me." This may seem like a perpetrator story, but I actually felt guilty, ashamed and paranoid as if at any moment a punitive God/Mother might pulverize me.

Like most children at the age of two, I thought the world revolved around me. I was just beginning to separate from my mother and form an ego. Perhaps because of the shoe incident and others like it, I became emotionally frozen in time. As I grew up, therefore, I made myself small and weak by bowing down to the power of my victim story. First, I compensated by being a "good girl," then switched tracks and became the "black sheep" of the family. All the while, I tried to find a role that made sense to me.

I had a hard time making good decisions because I was haunted by a subconscious panic that I'd done something wrong and I'd be punished by some hateful, monster-like deity who wanted to destroy me. "You are a miserable sinner!" it screamed. I had to escape it at all costs.

A more recent piece of my life's puzzle came when I was in my mid 30s. I'd married a wonderful man and settled into family life. During that time, I noticed that at about 10:00 in the morning, once my husband went to work and my daughter was at school, I'd start to feel anxious. After a while, I began questioning, "What is going on with me? Why am I so uptight? Why now and not an hour ago?"

Examining my feelings, I saw that when I was on my own for a few hours I felt tense because I didn't have the early morning distractions of taking care of everyone else. Tinged with a vague, uncomfortable feeling that I needed to do more and be more, I didn't feel adequate. I pushed myself to be better, to get more done and to accomplish something of value.

A voice constantly nagged at me saying, "I must have done something horribly wrong." It also said, "I should have saved Mom from herself, but I didn't. I failed."

Looking back to my birth, I realized that this pattern had set itself from the very beginning of this lifetime. Since I was conceived just two months after my brother passed away, I subconsciously assumed I was supposed to sweeten my parent's pain by giving them new life. But I couldn't do it. I faltered in a mission I wasn't sure I really wanted, later rebelled against and finally moved across the country to escape. With my mother's suicide, failure was inevitable. I couldn't save Mom, I couldn't save the world and, until I radically forgave, I couldn't save myself.

My victim story caused me to feel tremendous anxiety and guilt just about all the time. Thanks to a buffering wall of denial I scarcely realized this fact; nonetheless, these emotions lurked maliciously under the surface of my waking consciousness.

Once I found Radical Forgiveness and began studying *A Course in Miracles* (a spiritual text which explores forgiveness and its healing powers in an in-depth, masterful way), my story emerged from the deep recesses of my subconscious even more completely. I began to see that my mother's illness symbolized the split in my own mind: Life could be wonderful (caring Mom) then fall apart entirely (depressed, possessed Mom). I'd decided that good times couldn't be trusted. They'd just be followed by bad times. I felt trapped and helpless, because my victim story told me over and over I'd failed. Unconsciously, I felt I'd done something horribly wrong, and no mother and no Creator would ever take care of me. The earth underneath me couldn't hold me, and I'd never be good enough to deserve God's love.

Gradually, as I slowly surfaced from my habit of denial, my life patterns became clear. I saw how over time I had taught myself to plan ahead for disaster, becoming a world class worrier in the process. I married a man who doesn't fret—at least out loud, and this brought the decibel level of my silent worries up to a dim roar inside my head. Caught in an invisible net of dread, nothing felt quite right. Even when life flowed easily, I worried that soon, misfortune would arrive.

**Healing, Relief and Inspiration from the Divine**

To heal my experience with my mother, I needed to commit myself to the philosophy of forgiveness. I needed to pause, learn and take responsibility for all aspects of myself, including my relationship with abandonment and insanity. I had to release my ego's insistence upon duality and replace it with the truth about myself: I am lovable and I am love. To do this, I also needed to give myself a loving parent. I had to see myself as a loving and loved child of God.

By embracing all of my life experience—instead of desiring some of it and running from the rest, I began to see that my mother gave me love, a place to grow a physical body, nurturing, artistic talent, dance lessons, and so much more. She also gave me plenty of ways in which I could uncover my addiction to believing in my ego's voice as it nagged me with its victim stories. She offered me vast opportunities to contend with my own feelings of fear and helplessness. As eternal souls, she and I helped each other in this lifetime—even if it looked quite the opposite in the physical world.

For instance, as a focal point for my despair, anger and blame, I now see how my mother showed me how I refused to take responsibility for my emotional life. I'd kept most of this refusal unconscious and under thick layers of denial for years. I wasn't alone; this scenario describes a common strategy the ego uses to keep itself alive in most people. The mental places where I blamed myself and others were precisely the places where I hadn't yet forgiven. I could blame my mother because she'd attacked me when I was two years old, or because she had mental illness and it appeared she'd abandoned me. I could, and I have. It's easy. My mother didn't force me to keep telling my victim story to myself, though; she had passed on over 20 years ago. With the option of blame stripped away, I found myself alone with myself, my ego's voices and my desire for change.

At this point, I clearly saw some of the lessons my soul came to Earth to learn. I already knew that the experience of living with a mother who suffered from manic-depressive disorder affected my entire childhood. I couldn't count on her to "be there for me" and began (or, more accurately, continued) an internal story that the people I love will abandon me. Later, many other people I loved either left me or died. It seemed true: I was abandoned by those I cared for the most.

Using the technology of Radical Forgiveness, I began to contemplate how my mind had projected its fear-based thoughts upon the world. I felt so worried about being abandoned, yet I realized that on a soul level I may have attracted abandonment so I could learn from it and heal my misperception.

In *A Course in Miracles* I read, "What he is, is unaffected by his thoughts. But what he looks upon is their direct result." I was gently reminded that what I am is sacred, eternal and whole, though my misunderstanding about reality caused grave suffering in my life.

I looked underneath that trusty blanket of denial and explored the specific spots where I had abandoned myself and others. I asked myself where and when I'd been the crazy one, even if it was subtle or private or invisible to others. I demanded that I see how I'd left my true nature and abandoned my connection to God.

This process humbled me and taught me compassion. Once I'd seen how much I'd embodied the same energies of fear as my mother had during her mental illness, I could no longer separate myself from her in the same familiar way. Yes, she acted out in a dramatic way by taking her life, but I came to realize that histrionics don't matter much. Scale doesn't matter, either.

As souls, we either entertain our errors or we learn from them and heal them. Bringing myself to such a humble place taught me something more. Forgiveness felt great! I learned that humility is a good thing; it disarms the ego, and from that point new potential for health and wholeness comes to light.

## Coming Home

For me, forgiveness occurs when I realize I've abandoned love and truth and *I just want to come home*. I'm willing to do whatever it takes to see everyone involved as a child of God. I begin with prayer and honesty. Deep emotions follow and flow, loosening up all my misperceptions about myself and the world.

No matter what happened, no matter who was involved, whenever and wherever I was crazy — I exhale, forgive and let go. If someone appeared to abandon me, I forgive and let go. If I appeared to abandon someone, I forgive myself and let go. Seeing when and where the world seems insane, I say, yes, I know. I forgive and let go. I come home to God. Forgiveness is the bridge, leading us directly to the Holy Spirit. Its heart medicine makes all things new.

Forgiveness showed me a way to heal the pain and anguish I felt about my mother's illness and death. I needed someone to lean on who could nurture me with soft strength and sound advice. Humbly, I called out, "Help!" and, crossing the bridge, took all fear and anger to the merciful heart of the Goddess. I let my pain and sadness go into Her lap of love. It didn't happen all at once; this process took plenty of introspection, a few buckets of tears, volumes of spontaneous prayer, and a gradual shedding of layer upon layer of grief and memory. I called upon patience and the force of my will, combining them with the tender balm of Her blessing.

I let the Divine Mother lead me to peace. She seems invisible, yet I've found that She is trustworthy.

Through Radical Forgiveness, I learned to find the "gift in the situation" and to embrace my mother just as she was, just as she is — a divine, eternal being of Light…just like me.

From my new perspective, I see my mother's life and death as just what she needed for her awakening. She pointed me toward the Divine, and especially into the eternal care of the Divine Mother. With a huge sense of relief, I discovered that the Holy Spirit would never leave me even if my earthly mother needed to pass on. I could finally be at peace with all the events that happened, and even better, see how they served me in ways my soul desired for my liberation.

There are many reasons to forgive using this radical, spiritual and unapologetically universal philosophy. When we forgive using Radical Forgiveness, we do it for our own internal freedom. We do it because we crave Reality with a capital R, and Truth with a capital T. We forgive everyone, including ourselves, for the sake of all creation. We do it to heal our memories and begin again, to be born anew into this fresh and innocent moment.

Everyday I learn more about my connection with God. *A Course in Miracles* tells us that Reality is by its nature pure and loving. To meet it, we must match its love and purity of heart. That's all we need to do; the rest is already given. By releasing our sorrow and anger with forgiveness, we uncover the essence of self that lies patiently waiting. The Holy Spirit keeps the truth for us until we are ready to claim it as our own.

How ironic, or crazy, that I received such opposite messages about life during my childhood. My victim story convinced me that I'd done something horribly wrong, was abandoned by the ones I loved and that insanity was so terrifying I had to run away. At God's altar of love, I realize none of this is true. It was never true. In fact, as an eternal being, I haven't done anything wrong. I'm not abandoned or crazy. A higher truth emerges for me to embody: I AM completely and eternally innocent, healthy, connected and free.

When I believe this, I am absolutely at peace. If I stray for an instant, I immediately find myself flirting with fear and delusion. This is true for you, too, and for everyone on Earth. When we find the Truth, we know it to be the opposite of what we had previously thought was true.

My life with my mother taught me about the suffering that human beings endure. She also showed me that suffering takes many forms. Her mental illness took the guise of her suffering; growing up as her daughter formed mine. The other members of my family sculpted their versions as well, as does everyone in our greater human family. In the end, it is not only "my" suffering nor "yours" nor "my mother's" that needs healing, but the collective pain and fear that we must release if we want to find compassion and peace.

This compassion, also known as Divine Mother, offers me deep serenity and intuitive guidance. I realize that God has no gender, but sometimes it helps me to imagine my Creator as a gracious and loving mother. In my human frailty, reaching out to Divine Parents keeps me on track.

It provides me with an inner sense of safety and nurturance I rarely experienced as a child.

I am grateful and humbled by the sacred power and perfection of my life, no matter what happened, and no matter what will happen. This is my experience of peace and forgiveness. What a blessing!

**Finding Peace**

Recently, I found a beautiful box on a shelf, high up in the back of my closet. In it, I'd placed some old treasures which meant a lot to me, although I'd forgotten a few. To my surprise, inside the box I found a message from my mother in the form of a Hebrew prayer she'd handwritten for me shortly before her death.

Carefully scripted in Hebrew and in English, it read:


May the Lord bless thee and keep thee;

May the Lord make His face to shine upon thee,

And be gracious unto thee;

May the Lord lift up His countenance upon thee,

And give thee peace.

Numbers VI, 24-26

"Thanks, Mom," I thought, gazing at the page. "Go with God, and peace be with you, too."

# 4: Thawing a Frozen Heart

A Story of Awakening and Forgiveness

## By Julie Jones

The vacation my husband and I took to the captivating Galapagos Islands constituted the trip of a lifetime. It also served as a diversion; our 16-year marriage had died, but I had not faced up to that fact yet. Little did I know this trip represented the beginning of an exciting journey of uncovering the truths in my life and in my relationships. However, I had to look death in the eyes to begin my awakening.

We both loved adventure, and the islands provided us with many opportunities for exciting activity. For instance, on one particular day we went snorkeling. Despite the fact that a large bull sea lion lived across the bay—bull sea lions are the most dangerous animals in the Galapagos—the tour guides told us that we could snorkel safely as long as we stayed on our side of the bay. They lied.

Late in the afternoon, just two of us remained in the water. After my last snorkeling run, I raised my head from the water and heard an ear-shattering and angry bellow. I looked across the bay. The bull sea lion and I locked eyes for a split second before he shot off in my direction like a rocket. I immediately started swimming frantically to shore. Every time I snuck a peek behind me, it became more obvious that the huge animal had made me his target and was closing in quickly. His enraged roar sent shock waves through my body and confirmed the fact that a 600-pound beast was swimming 17 miles per hour towards me.

Almost to shore, waist deep in the surf and screaming bloody hell, I took off my fins so I could possibly move faster, but I realized I was not going to make it to safety in time. Holding my flimsy fins in front of me for protection, I turned to face the bull sea lion.

At a distance of just three feet, I looked into the face of certain death—one distorted by rage, baring its teeth in an open red slash of mouth. I felt my body unconsciously freeze, shutting down as it prepared for pain and the end of life. Suddenly, two tour guides magically ran up on either side of me, yelling and slapping the water with their life jackets. The beast stopped, closed his red snarling mouth, dropped down into the water, and swam slowly out to sea. I collapsed and the guides carried me out of the water.

I did not realize at that moment that when I looked into the piercing eyes of the bull sea lion, I looked into my past and into the issues I needed to heal.

**My Journey Begins**

I held myself together for the rest of the trip with false bravado and a frozen smile. No more snorkeling, of course, but lots of safe hiking on the islands. Determined to document the perfect trip, I hid my trauma behind my camera lens while photographing every bit of flora and fauna. At night, I experienced something different. The image of the bull sea lion's angry eyes filled my dreams, and I awakened in a nauseous cold sweat with my heart beating wildly.

I could not hide my feelings on the long and horrendous flight home. Pure, constant terror made every nerve in my body pulsate. My eyes felt like bulging orbs in my head as I mentally watched the scene over and over, seeing that monster barreling down on me as if he were doing so in that moment again. I unconsciously shuddered, trying to shake the images out of my head, but it did not work.

I used my brain to try to minimize the incident by thinking, "You're safe now. It is over. Relax. Don't be a baby." That tactic always had worked throughout my life, but my heart and body did not listen this time. I felt exposed and out of control. I had survived the attack, but I did not feel safe or sane. I began to fear I was having a nervous breakdown. Little did I know I was experiencing a breakthrough instead. My frozen facade of denial, perfectionism and control, which I had worn all my life, had melted away in the Galapagos waters. I just did not know it yet.

When I returned to the United States, I remained in a state of shock. Even home felt unsafe now. I remained in a constant state of alert and agitation, my senses on edge. The smallest noise startled me. I responded as if still in danger, always calculating how much time I had left to escape and save myself from impending doom.

## Pandora's Box Opens

Unable to handle the effects of my traumatic experience, I made an appointment with a therapist soon after I returned home. The attack had shattered my illusion of being in control and able to handle anything by myself. In pain and desperate for relief, something snapped in me before I could even make it to my first appointment. Not only did I realize I felt anger and outrage by this unprovoked and random attack, my heightened senses and acute rage opened my eyes to something else going on in my life.

I had ignored warning signs that pointed to the possibility that my husband was cheating on me for a long time. I now suddenly found the gumption to investigate and confront him with my findings. He admitted the truth. Thus, I found myself at my first appointment with the therapist talking not about the bull sea lion attack, but about my dissolving marriage.

I had to admit, though, that while my husband had led a secret life, I had, too. A couple of months before our trip, I secretly started drinking again after 13 years of white-knuckled sobriety. I had become depressed even before our trip as I realized the two of us were drifting farther and farther apart. Then, my facade of a perfect and happy marriage melted away in the Galapagos waters.

I saw my therapist every week and discovered my denial went far beyond my marriage. Before the trip to the Galapagos Islands, I believed I had had an idyllic childhood with perfect parents. Therapy helped me see that the bull sea lion incident had opened a Pandora's box filled with events from my past and repressed feelings of terror, anger and depression due to early trauma. For me to heal, I had to face the painful truth about my childhood. Slowly, over many therapy sessions, I unraveled my past.

Outside my childhood home, the world saw a perfect family with smiley faces, but a different and dark reality existed inside the house. Most families thought of spanking as an innocent and accepted punishment in the 1950s. Yet, my parents did not spank me; they beat me. At least three times a week, my dad or mom—or both, left welts on my skinny body with belts, switches from hedges and hairbrushes for the most minor infractions. These beatings hurt physically, but the angry look in their eyes hurt more. A typical week included many unexpected slaps across the face as well. Thus, I lived in constant terror.

My parents also shamed me severely with constant emotional and verbal abuse. My dad used vicious sarcasm and demeaning words. My mother treated me like a puppet on a string, controlling my every word and movement. She managed to kill every one of my ambitions and dreams outside of the family.

On the other hand, my mother fussed over me and dressed me up like a Shirley Temple doll. She expected me to look and act perfect. These served as my marching orders into adulthood. I grew up unable to feel; I grew up afraid to fail, afraid to succeed, afraid to show emotions, afraid of just about everything. I became frozen emotionally, but unconsciously I felt shame and rage.

As soon as I could—at age 14—I started drinking to escape the pain. I passed out the first time I drank. I coped by abusing alcohol. When I stopped drinking at age 43, I replaced alcohol with controlling and judging others along with an unhealthy dose of perfectionism.

Continued therapy revealed to me an even more painful truth—a shocking, buried secret. My dad had sexually abused me as a toddler. Not only did my dad molest me, but my mom did not protect me from him. I never knew from where my chronic obsession with masturbation came, but now I understood. My parents shamed me in front of the family for this "bad habit," but my dad caused it. This stunning revelation shook me to the core. All this time I had blamed myself, but in reality, my parents had served as the perpetrators.

The most profound damage to me occurred at the age of four. Despite the physical abuse, I used to wait breathlessly at the front door for my dad to come home from work. The highlight of my day came when he swept me up in his arms and carried me around while I wrapped my arms about his neck. One day this daily event came to a crushing halt. He arrived home cold and withdrawn. He did not respond to my outstretched arms. He looked at me with disgust and walked away. His eyes scared me. Instead of loving and soft, they were mean and hard, like the eyes of the bull sea lion.

I waited at the front door each day after that, yearning for my happy relationship with my father to return, but it never did. My dad never again picked me up or hugged me lovingly. Whether my mother found out about his visits to my bedroom and forbade him to touch me, or this served as his way of stopping himself from abusing me, I do not know. I only know that I was a precious, loved girl one day and a disgusting unloved girl the next, and that broke my heart. Unknowingly, at that time I made up my mind never to love anyone with all my heart and get hurt like that again. My heart froze, and I learned to clamp on a frozen smiley face to go with it.

## Opening the Door to Healing

After exposing my childhood wounds, my therapist gently led me through a process to feel and release the toxic emotions of helpless anger, numbing depression and paralyzing fear I still held in my body. I acknowledged my abusive past and the damage it caused in my life. Through the painful process, I began to see glimpses of what life could be like with an open heart and without the burden of my past. However, still feeling a victim of the past, I boiled in a cauldron of bitterness and rage against my parents. I could not forgive them.

A year passed after the bull sea lion attack, and despite all my hours of therapy, my past continued to suffocate me. My dad had died several years before—an early death accelerated by alcoholism. While he was alive, my relationship with him remained cordial, but distant and tense. Hearing the family lore about his humor and his love of beer made me seethe, because he left behind a legacy of cruel humor and alcoholism along with an undercurrent of violence.

My mother remains alive and well. Before my trip to the Galapagos, our adult relationship remained close and enmeshed with no boundaries. As my best friend, we spoke several times a day. After I unearthed my childhood truths, though, I could not stand to talk or visit with her. My new knowledge created anger and disdain for her within me, because she seemed to epitomize the codependency in our family of addicts. She used fear of failure and guilt to keep her family near her instead of encouraging our independence and success. She remained unaware that her controlling ways produced generation after generation of underachievers and addicts. I wanted her to see her role in this perfect family illusion. I wanted her to change.

Yet, I also did not want to carry this hateful bile of mine to the grave. I did not want to live the rest of my life hating my dead father and elderly mother like a snarling, raging teenager. I did not want to remain a bitter and resentful woman, but I could not forgive my abusers like a saint. My heart hurt constantly as if in the grip of a vise. I had opened the Pandora's box about my past, and I could not close it now. I heard Jack Nicholson's words ringing in my ears in the movie, "A Few Good Men," when he said, "You can't handle the truth!" I knew I had to learn how to do just that.

When I reached the point where the abuse I had suffered made me feel like the most pathetic victim on the planet, I asked my therapist, "Now what do I do with this hate and resentment? How can I possibly forgive my parents?"

She said, "I know about a program called Radical Forgiveness that can help you." She recommended I attend a "Making Room for the Miracle" weekend workshop and spoke highly of Colin Tipping, the founder of the Radical Forgiveness program. My therapist explained that this form of forgiveness could help me let go of my victim mentality by seeing my parents and other relationships in a new light.

## Letting It All Out

Radical Forgiveness teaches that childhood abuse, such as the abuse I had suffered, comprises part of a spiritual "big-picture plan" to help a person heal. Although thinking of my childhood as part of a spiritual plan seemed like a hard pill to swallow, I yearned for peace and an open, loving heart. So, I headed out to the beautiful Georgia hills north of Atlanta to the "Miracles" weekend, hoping and praying for exactly that—a miracle.

Nervous and tense on the ride from the airport, I immediately relaxed as we drove into the wooded and peaceful grounds of the retreat center. I felt safe immediately. Colin greeted us and invited us simply to become open to the possibility of Radical Forgiveness. I could do that. Certainly, the traditional way of forgiving my parents had failed me.

To leave "Victimland," as Colin called it, we needed to process our victim story through the five stages of Radical Forgiveness: 1) Telling the Story; 2) Feeling the Feelings; 3) Collapsing the Story; 4) Reframing the Story; and 5) Integration. Feeling and expressing my raw feelings in a group setting intimidated me. Sometimes called anger work, Colin explained that this process simply moved stuck energy through and out of the body by surrendering to our emotions. I had already done similar work with my therapist, but I still suffered from a ton of leftover rage.

I certainly did not want to scream and hit a pillow in front of a group. As a child, if I showed an inkling of anger toward my parents, they punished me. Thus, I learned to hide my anger and control my emotions behind an

93

emotionless face. Controllers like me do not like to surrender, scream and beat pillows. To me, being angry felt out of control. That terrified me, but it seemed necessary to get unstuck.

Ironically, the first step out of Victimland called us to revisit feeling like a victim by telling our story while expressing our painful emotions. Despite my fear, when it came time to beat that pillow, I allowed myself to remember the slashing pain of dad's belt hitting my skin, and I let it rip. I screamed. I cried. I whined. I raged. I spat out expletives. "Damn you, damn you both. I hate you, hate you, hate you. You hurt me. You hurt me so bad. Not fair, not fair. I'm just a little girl. Why? Why? I'm so scared. I want to be free. I just want to be free. I want to run away. I want to die. I want you to die. You don't love me."

I wallowed in my victim story, crying and feeling all the pent-up rage, pain and terror that gripped my heart. Exhausted and trembling after what seemed like a long time, I finally stopped raging. My heart felt only emptiness and sadness. Weeping and lying prostrate on the pillow, my life passed in front of me. "Dad, you killed my soul and sense of safety. Your cruelty and rejection almost destroyed me and kept me from being a whole, loving woman. I'm an alcoholic who squashed her feelings and squandered her life just like you. Mom, not only did you abuse me, but you did not protect me from Dad. Controlling and judgmental, you discounted me. You still do not accept me for who I am. Because of you, I am an uptight perfectionist who is afraid to succeed," I yelled. Through my tears, a chant automatically spilled out of my mouth: "I just wanted love, I just wanted love, I just wanted love."

Lying there, spent, I realized all my thoughts boiled down to one simple and stunning belief: I was unlovable. After all, my dad did not want me, and my mother loved me only if I was perfect. All my life I harbored a false belief that kept my heart frozen so I could not love or accept others and myself. That simple lightning bolt of awareness caused my heart to pulsate with hope. Freed from the icy grip of anger and fear, in that moment my heart started to thaw, opening to love and life.

This epiphany stunned and at the same time freed me. Although my parents abused me as a child, I had held myself back all my life, because I viewed myself as unlovable. Now surely I could do something about my false belief. I began to see that a way existed out of this victim cage.

Moving on to the third step, collapsing the story, Colin taught us about a principle called "mirroring." Colin described it in one succinct sentence, "If you spot it, you got it." In this process, we identify the qualities that we hate in other people that cause us to get upset or self-righteous. Those represent the qualities we hate about ourselves but do not acknowledge. I had no trouble naming the qualities I hated about my parents.

My dad withheld love, affection and affirmation. He put down people behind their backs using cruel and demeaning humor. He masked his feelings behind alcohol. My mom, the master manipulator, knew all the answers. As a control freak, she judged everyone behind her angelic smile. My parents offered me love only if I was good and perfect. If I did not comply, they became vindictive and withheld their love and approval. They both squelched my ambitions.

95

Suddenly, I stopped listing their negative qualities. The meaning of "If you spot it, you got it" sank into my consciousness. "Oh, my God, I am my parents. That's the way I treat myself and others." I saw my dark, shadowy side, the qualities I hated in myself that I never acknowledged. These characteristics stifled me all my life. It was like watching a horror movie, and suddenly seeing myself as the monster up on the screen. I hated admitting the truth to myself. I felt embarrassed, angry and humiliated.

Colin led us further down the path to escape Victimland. Still stinging after seeing myself so vividly as my parents, my heart and eyes began to open further. I thought I was ready for whatever came next. And, boy, was it radical!

Colin said my parents had been sent into my life to heal me. In other words, on a soul level I co-created the abusive situation with them so I could grow spiritually. He expected me somehow to believe that — at the soul level — my parents unselfishly sacrificed themselves for my growth. He asked me to see the situation as perfect, like a Divine plan guiding my life. "You have to be kidding," I thought. My pride and outrage flared up. I had worked so hard to admit the imperfection of my childhood, and now he was asking me to see the perfection in it.

"Just be open to the possibility," Colin said. I grimaced at the idea of taking this big leap of faith.

**The Worksheet Works**

Radical Forgiveness uses many tools, but the Radical Forgiveness Worksheet constitutes a key element. At this point in the weekend, Colin asked us to complete worksheets on those people we wanted to forgive. By doing so, I found myself taking my victim story through the final stages toward forgiveness. To heal, I had to look figuratively into the eyes of my attackers—my parents—and bless them for playing a part in my healing as if they had done nothing wrong. With Colin's refrain of, "Fake it 'til you make it," I reluctantly filled out a worksheet on my father.

Dubious about how filling out a piece of paper could release me from Victimland, I summarized my victim story and raw feelings on the worksheet. By the time I reached the forgiveness section of the exercise, where I was asked to reframe, collapse and integrate my new story, my words began flowing. I was faking it until I could make it, but a funny thing happened while faking it. Without even realizing it, my perspective shifted as I wrote to my dad.

"Dad, I now see that you were in my life to teach me to love without fear of being abandoned," I wrote. "You abused me, and it taught me not to continue that vicious cycle of abuse under the guise of discipline with my own daughter. You were willing to sacrifice your life to an early death by alcohol so I would stop drinking. You could have enjoyed a fulfilling and creative life, but you settled for less to show me I could thrive creatively. Most of all, Dad, thank you for showing me that I am lovable and free. You took on the role of the bad person so I could heal and ratchet up my awakening in this lifetime. I know how difficult a role you played, and I know you are my healing angel. I forgive you. I hope you are at peace. I am." I looked back on the words that I had written and cried softly with relief.

Next, I started a worksheet on my mother. Since she remained in my life trying to control and manipulate me, I was reluctant even to think about forgiving her. However, my resistance melted when I remembered how my dark traits mirrored hers. "Ouch," I thought, "How the truth can hurt." So, with pen in hand, I addressed my mother.

"Mom, you were willing to be the villainess by stifling me so I could find true self-acceptance and self-love when I blossomed late in life. I needed that painful childhood so I could become a creative and sensitive writer and help others with my words," I wrote. "Without my victim story, I had no story to tell. By understanding your fear of failure and success, I feel free now to live a life full of passion and purpose. I forgive you. Thank you for being a healing angel by mirroring the dark traits I suppressed. You helped me see that unconditional love for myself and others is beautiful and freeing."

I had difficulty really forgiving my mother, though. While I could find the willingness to say I forgave her and accepted her, my heart was not quite into it—not at that moment. It would take many worksheets to reach that point, but I knew my salvation depended on reaching that point.

Umbilical cord severed, freed from the weight of the self-imposed block of ice around my heart, I felt like running through the Georgia woods shouting, "I'm free, I'm free." I now clearly saw how my parents, whom I demonized as ruining my life, actually aided my spiritual healing and growth. I felt compassion for them, because they played such cruel roles. I felt compassion for the limited lives they led so I might have a full life. Now, with a sense of responsibility for my own life and healing, I realized a full life, indeed, awaited me.

## One More to Forgive

Then Colin threw me for a loop. He said, "Julie, I invite you to do a worksheet on the bull sea lion."

I said to him, "Now that's weird! How do you forgive a crazed killing machine?" Somehow, I could not picture my soul sitting down with the soul of a bull sea lion and plotting who was going to eat whom. However, I was willing to give it a shot.

First, Colin asked me to stand up in front of the group and tell my story. I also had to express my real feelings about the attack. Feeling a little silly at first, I realized as I told the story that I felt damned mad. The ugly beast came after me for no reason and almost killed me, not only ruining the vacation of a lifetime, but also traumatizing me. It emphasized my belief that safety exists nowhere and people lie when they say it does. For this reason, I must stay hyper-vigilant and fearful at all times.

As I stood in front of the group, it dawned on me, "Wait, I have been hyper-vigilant and fearful all my life." Stunned, I realized that I needed the bull sea lion attack to recognize the other bull sea lions in my life.

The patterns in my life flashed in front of me. Starting with my parents and continuing with boyfriends, my first husband and my current husband, I had attracted people into my life that abandoned or abused me. They all confirmed my belief that I was unlovable. My fear of abandonment and hurt prevented me from feeling or loving. I chose to exist frozen and unloved. It took a real bull sea lion to finally get my attention. I needed to learn my life lesson: not to stay paralyzed and turn away from love and life, because I am lovable. The bull sea lion's laser eyes actually had begun the process of thawing my frozen heart.

Dumbfounded and speechless, I sat down. Picking up a worksheet, I realized I had reached a state of spiritual awareness impossible to experience without the attack. Not a random and unfortunate event that scarred my vacation and scared the living daylights out of me, it happened so I could wake up and heal.

Writing to the bull sea lion on the worksheet, I said, "You forced me to confront my husband and delve into my past so I could heal. Because of you, I am no longer a helpless victim of my parents. Thank you for leaving your side of the bay to awaken me. I bless you. I forgive you. You are my healing angel."

I could not help but laugh at the vision of a bull sea lion decked out in angel's wings, flying across the bay. The bull sea lion initiated my heart's escape out of the icy cage that surrounded it.

**Making Room for the Miracle**

My life changed dramatically from that moment on. I no longer lived in the past nor blamed my parents. I no longer withdrew from love and ruined relationships with my fear. This new perspective—that all the events in my life happened for a reason—melted the bitterness I harbored towards my parents. I became less judgmental and controlling. My relationship with my husband healed. I now enjoy passion in my life. I found true joy, because I live a life without secrets. I learned to give love unconditionally, and I am open to receiving love.

My awakening started with a dramatic event. Not many people snorkeling peacefully in the water on a beautiful island become the target of an unprovoked bull sea lion attack, but nothing less would have awakened me. Oblivious to subtle messages, I could not have responded to a gentle seal playfully popping out of the water. Some wake-up calls happen because of a tragic accident or illness. I feel fortunate that my earth-shattering awakening did not involve maiming in the process.

Yet, you do not have to wait for a bull sea lion attack to awaken. You can do so by looking at the patterns in your life and applying the Radical Forgiveness principles. You do not have to look into the killer eyes of a bull sea lion. Just look at your life with open eyes.

It takes only five simple words to get started: make room for the miracle. If hating your parents and being miserable no longer works for you, then you have nothing to lose except drama and unhappiness. Trying to forgive my parents the traditional way left me bitter and frustrated, because I could not release the past. Applying the Radical Forgiveness concept—that I picked my parents on a soul level so they could teach me life lessons—brought true forgiveness and peace into my life. Realizing that one fact alone changed my life. You can change your life by understanding this fact, too.

Although I left the workshop with a major shift in perception about my parents, I sometimes fall back into old patterns of resentment. I work it out by using the Radical Forgiveness tools, which pull me back into balance. I have completed many worksheets on my parents since leaving the workshop. Just like exercising to keep my body in shape, I use the Radical Forgiveness tools to maintain radical forgiveness in my life. I continue to grow by seeing traits from my dark side mirrored in my mother and in other people.

My relationship with my mother gets better every day. I have had to set boundaries with her. Her resentment of my independence made this difficult. We have a different relationship now, because I see her in light of Radical Forgiveness. Although challenging, I have set my goal simply to accept her as she is—without needing her to change. I now realize that I did not have the right to demand that my parents love me unconditionally. They did not know how. More importantly, my dad was on his own journey, and my mother's life is her business.

This shift in perspective I experienced felt like an earthquake when it first occurred, and it still reverberates throughout my life. Today, I live a full and passionate life. My husband went to the Radical Forgiveness workshop, and the rift in our marriage healed. We understand each other better because of Radical Forgiveness. New pieces of the puzzle of my life appear when I pay attention to coincidences, patterns and my intuition. My life now may not be as dramatic as confronting a speeding bull sea lion, but I live it just as powerfully.

You may wish you had other parents. I did. You may be miserable because you hate your parents. I was. You may blame your parents for everything wrong in your life. I did. Yet, you do not have to live a life of bitterness and regret. You can heal your wounds. You can forgive your parents and yourself, enriching your current relationships in the process. You can be free to live a life of joy, peace and passion. You can make way for the miracle. I did. You can, too.

# 5: The Moment of Truth

*Reality Isn't Always Real*

## By Bella Rose Fontaine

I once thought I possessed a rather unique personal story. In a world filled with billions of people I felt alone. How ironic. Years later, I found solace in the realization that many people have had similar life experiences to my own. Indeed, I now am hard pressed to find people who have *not* experienced some sort of trauma or abuse at some point in their lives. What a humbling yet disturbing epiphany.

Given this fact, I could describe the world as sad and bleak, but I won't. Nothing is as it was, and nothing ever is as it seems. Just like the hands of time, everything shifts and changes. The same goes for perception, and mine has changed dramatically. There comes a time in your life when you realize that the truth does not necessarily constitute the truth as you know it. Truth tends to be more of a personal thing, shaped and formed from how we see and perceive the world around us, rarely based on reality.

I recently learned this life lesson, one of the most powerful I've learned to date in reclaiming a sense of power I thought I had lost. Truth, or truth as we know it, formed

103

by our deeply rooted beliefs into something that did not necessarily exist, shapes our personal story. It seems real and we call it "reality," but it may just be "perceived reality." Our experiences then become "our" truth, but not necessarily "the" truth. I call this "the veil of illusion." As one layer of the veil lifts away, another reveals itself.

## Where It All Began

I grew up on a farm in a small prairie community where everything seemed perfect on the outside. I had a loving father and mother and two younger brothers with whom to play. I remember being a joyous, playful and sometimes mischievous child with a curiosity about life and a love for everything around me. I danced under sunny skies of blue, rolled down grassy slopes of green, ran through golden fields of wheat, laughed so hard I cried, and took pride each day that I helped out on the farm as much as a little person could. Each day felt like a breath of fresh air. I led a beautiful simple life where I only worried about not falling out of the apple trees or trying to keep the sand within the sandbox. I knew of nothing different; life couldn't have been more grand.

Things aren't always as they seem, though. In 1988, a month before my eighth birthday, my perfect utopian world fell around me in one swift movement when my parents divorced. Like a prairie tornado that hits under the guise of night, I woke up to find my home gone, and I was left choking in the dust to deal with the debris.

With my world suddenly turned upside-down, I had to adjust to a new town, a new school, half a home, and unfamiliar people in an unfamiliar place. I felt angry, hurt, cheated, alone, abandoned, betrayed, and incomplete. I was thrown into a reality from which I wanted to run, a role I never wanted, and a life for which I never signed up. I remained a child on the outside but was forced into adulthood within. My new reality felt more like a bad dream, and I hoped I'd wake from it soon.

## To Hell and Back—The Years That Haunted Me

At the age of 28, I wrote a college term paper that discussed a life event of momentous impact. This branching point took place in my teen years and writing about it influenced my life significantly. The following is an excerpt of that assignment. It serves as a reflection of my broken heart and my world as I saw it *then* — and I stress *then*, not now. It was 1994; I was 13 going on 14

> …excited about moving in with my dad and his new wife before my 14th birthday. My mom always told us that we had to wait until we were 13 years old before we could decide to move out and go live with our dad. The time had come. It seemed I had been waiting for this moment my whole life. I had spent years crying over a dad who never seemed to be around or lived too far to visit. I needed him. I longed to be "daddy's little girl" again the way it used to be – how naïve. When the time came, I willfully abandoned those who were there for me most—my mom and two brothers—only to be abandoned by those with whom I chose to live—my dad and his new wife. I learned to be careful what I wished for…sometimes you get more than what you bargained for.

I enjoyed my first six months at my dad's home. All was well, as long as I didn't step out of line. However, life events happened, and circumstances for my dad and step mom changed drastically along with the family dynamics. I soon became the proverbial doormat, and my life started spiraling downward. Anger, frustration and resentment from my parents filled the air, and I got the brunt of it.

To compensate I strove for perfection. I figured, if I am perfect then I can do no wrong, and I am safe. At least so I thought. With a life that much resembled that of a modern day "Cinderella," I felt taken advantage of and became resentful. Nothing I did seemed enough or right. I fought a losing battle. Their words of abuse, criticisms, rejection, mindless commentary, hurtful jests, belittling, and even insulting me about my sexual development took its toll on me, leaving me emotionally and psychologically wounded. Most days I lived in fear. My pillow comforted tears of sadness and hurt and silenced my screams of anger and deep resentment. I feared punishment and retribution if I dared express these emotions, yet my father's and step-mother's own expressions of anger towards me became more than I could bear.

Unable to find the love, appreciation, and acceptance for which I longed, I soon opted for apathy and became reluctant to even try to make the situation better. Being the good girl got me nowhere, so I figured, "Why bother?" Pain and disappointment burdened my heart, and a deep hatred for my father and his new wife grew along with disgust for myself. "I never bargained for this!" I thought.

Oh, wait...I did. The saying, "You made your bed, now lie in it," comes to mind. Even I had a hard time imagining why I'd actually chosen this living situation. A sucker for punishment—or a perpetual optimistic, I stayed another year hoping things would change.

In 1996, we moved to a bigger house within the same town, where nothing changed but the scenery and an increase of my stressors. At the age of 16, I took on the responsibility of being a young mother without actually birthing any children. For the years that followed, caring for and disciplining my little brother and sister stole my desire to ever become a mother; I had already been one. Kids shouldn't have to discipline kids, but my parents made me do so, causing my innocence to vanish like the wind.

I felt disgusting, dirty and wrong, and I hated the monster I had become. No better than my parents, I now hated myself even more. Sweet sixteen wasn't so sweet. I wrote in my essay:

> *The stress became more than I could handle. My father and stepmother constantly put me down for how I looked physically, for singing, for playing the flute (which I loved), and called me lazy and stupid. I couldn't do anything right. I just wanted to belong somewhere, to feel wanted and to be special to someone, yet I was treated dramatically different than "her" kids. I felt very left out and didn't really belong to either family anymore. Frustrated and angry, I wanted to scream. I felt dispensable and deprived of my both my childhood and of love. And if that wasn't enough, as punishment my father and stepmother took away my only source of sanity and solace—my best friend. That was the last straw.*
>
> *I snapped. My pain and rage became so intense it colored my world red. I spent every night drowning my tears in music, writing my anguish in a journal,*

*beating my pillow with fists of rage, feeling life being choked out of me.*

*"So this is what hate feels like," I write, as thoughts I've never had before creep into my brain. I consider anything to stop the pain and craziness. I wish death upon my dad and stepmom, and I fantasize about doing it. I only wanted to kill her, though. She represented the main source of my pain. My father, pussy-whipped and spineless, just sat on the sidelines and watched me go through my ordeal. I considered Dad a failure as a father—a major disappointment.*

*The thought of going to jail stopped me from following through on my murderous thoughts. "How is it fair that I be punished twice? Isn't living with them sentence enough," I questioned. That left just one option. "One of us has to go," I concluded.*

*Suicide seemed my answer. "That'll make them pay," I thought. "I want them to feel my pain, my anguish. I want them to know that they did this to me, and I want them to rot in hell for it and feel as low as I do. I want to make them feel small and like failures. I want to show them how fucked up they are and show the world how fucking horrible they were to me. I want people to know how ugly their hearts are and that all is not as it appears on the outside."*

*I fantasized about them finding me swinging from the rafters. "Maybe then they'll get that I'm serious," I thought. "They don't seem to give a fuck otherwise."*

*I thought it out. I was scared but ready to die. I didn't see any other way.*

*I picked out a beam in the basement and planned it out. I thought about using the vacuum cord, but didn't think it would be strong enough. So, I looked for a rope instead. I couldn't find one. I thought about going to a hardware store to buy one.*

The moments that followed next continue to remain a mystery to me; they must have been an act of God, I think. On my way to the hardware store after school, my best friend, who knew nothing of my plans but only of my hardships, asked me if would consider talking to the school counselor. I must have said, "Yes," because I soon found myself sitting in a small room with her and the counselor. There I spilled it all. I spent two or three hours after school that day recounting my story to the counselor, bawling my eyes out, barfing out everything I'd held in for so long. I knew I wasn't crazy when my counselor cried, too. That was all the validation I needed.

*I waited until the end of the school year before I moved back in with my mom. As my stuff was loaded into the truck, my father still managed to make me feel guilty for my decision—as if it were all my fault. "Just wait and see," Dad said "You'll thank us some day."*

**Lesson Continued until a Lesson Learned**

Ten years—10 *whole* years—had passed since I moved out of my father's house, and I still carried deep hurt, anger and resentment within for had what happened there—more accurately for what I *perceived* had happened there. Ten years. That represented more than a third of my life.

I spent the majority of that decade on the move and usually far away from family. I didn't really do this consciously or on purpose, but I did feel compelled to "get away," as they say. So I did. I moved, traveled and accepted jobs out of the country so I could live the life I wanted and create a clean slate for myself where ever I went. No one knew me, no one had to know me and they would only know me as I created myself. I felt safe and free to be me—or so I thought.

In reality, however, only the location truly changed; all else remained the same. The "systems" or beliefs I had about myself in my teen years ran my show and kept influencing me like a bad habit. Negative thoughts, like "I'm not good enough" or "You can't hurt me," lived in my life like old, unwanted friends who kept rearing their ugly heads.

At a certain point in your life, though, you stop running I didn't know it at the time, but that point came when I turned 27. Things hadn't been going well for me, and I was offered the chance to move one more time. Since I felt the Universe had been saying "No" to most of what I desired, I decided to say "Yes" to this opportunity. So, I found myself packing my bags again and heading for the West Coast, a move that once again would place me as far away from home as I could get without drowning in the sea.

As life would have it, my journey led me back to school in 2008—not any ordinary school though but an experiential coaching and counseling school. In the midst of all my recent career changes I had discovered a passion for wanting to help others excel in life and live the life of their dreams with genuine enthusiasm and love. I didn't often see people accomplishing this goal, but I knew I possessed a gift that helped them do so. I decided I wanted to work with children and to build them up rather than to take them down. This seemed fitting given my own childhood experiences.

I chose the school I attended rather naively, not really knowing much about it. I began my studies with no real idea what lay ahead. If I had known at the time, I probably wouldn't have gone to the first class. For once, ignorance, indeed, was bliss. In class I learned a great deal about myself and started my healing journey. In that school, a friend of mine introduced me to a book called *Radical Forgiveness* and its life-transforming content.

*"Radical Forgiveness?"* I wondered if this constituted some hokey-pokey idea. It took me about five months to actually buy the book. Like a bottle of vodka to an alcoholic, when I decided to crack it open, I drank up each page of this book with just as much vigor. I couldn't read it fast enough. I just had to read another page, and then another, until I finished the whole book.

The insights I received were akin to thinking and living your whole life as a blind person when you simply needed to open your eyes to see. Suddenly the world didn't seem so dark. I now could see the "furniture" on which I kept stubbing my toes. The old adage, "When the student is ready, the teacher appears," applies well here. When I picked up that book, I was ready for the lesson it offered.

Figuring I had nothing more to lose and sick of being the victim, in the fall of 2008, I decided to do the work and try a Radical Forgiveness Worksheet on my stepmom—11 years after the original pain. After all, I carried the most pain around my relationship with her. Quite amazingly,

111

without meaning to be cliché, it radically changed my life forever. Here's how my worksheet looked and how my process went:

### Making Room for the Miracle:

### A Radical Forgiveness Worksheet

**Date:** *September 6, 2008*

**Subject***: My stepmom for mal-treatment when I was younger*

**The situation around which I have an upset was:** *when I was a teenager. When I moved in with my dad and my stepmom I felt emotionally and verbally abused by her and insulted and hurt over all the negative condescending, mean comments towards me. I also felt used by her and that all I was good for was to work and serve her needs and those of her kids. I never felt valued, loved or appreciated for who I was, nor celebrated in my accomplishments. She just put me down a lot.*

**(Stepmom's name), I am upset with you because:** *you hurt my feelings and made me feel worthless, like I was less than your kids and that I was ugly, annoying, lazy, troublesome, and not good enough. Nothing I did was good or good enough. You used me.*

**Because of what you did:** *I have low self-esteem, low self-worth, shame, guilt, sadness, hurt anger, frustration, apathy, low self-confidence, pain, empty,* *lonely, betrayal, hopeless, feel less than others, and want more.*

Not really feeling the full impact of what I had written, I decided to delve a little deeper and be more specific. I made myself go through and fully feel each of the emotions I had written down so I would have a full understanding and clearer picture of why I even wrote the words in the first place. As I expanded upon the process, I wrote down exactly *why* I felt that way for each. The experience was even more powerful and really hit home for me, bringing everything back to life again as if the events and emotions had occurred just yesterday. Tears began to flow from the mere memories and the pain still trapped within. I found out the following by breaking down Question 2(b):

### *I felt:*

a. *Low self-esteem from all the negative comments*
b. *Low self-worth because what I did never seemed to matter*
c. *Shame because I feel there's something wrong with me*
d. *Guilt for feeling angry and telling this story*
e. *Sadness because I want the close family connection and love*
f. *Hurt that those I love choose to act this way*
g. *Anger that it happened*
h. *Frustration from feeling hopeless about change*
i. *Apathy in thinking nothing will change*
j. *Less than when my stepmom compares me*

*to others*
*k. Low self-confidence in feeling wrong or bad*
  *all the time*
*l. Pain from lack of love*
*m Emptiness from lack of loving feelings*
*n. Lonely because I feel like an outsider*
*o. Betrayal that family could choose to hurt*
  *and that I was turned against*
*p. Hopeless that my attempts to create change*
  *and a better family togetherness seem futile*
  *and stalemate*
*q. Wanting more because of the lack of family*
  *togetherness and solidarity*

Thankfully though, I found myself at a point in my life where the desire for change was far greater than the pain of staying the same. I had held onto these feelings with a vice-like death grip for far too long, and I knew my freedom and peace lay just on the other side of them. I wanted the possibility of something better than I had to date. So I let go.

For the first time I was willing to look at my own feelings and to take ownership of them. I'm not going to lie though; a part of me wanted to stand my ground and hold onto making my parents wrong for everything. But I'd already tried that and nothing had changed, so what would have been the point? Albert Einstein once said, doing the same thing over and over expecting different results is the definition of insanity. I think he was onto something. Being right kept everything the same and me feeling like a victim. Like a guest who stays just a little too long, the role of "victim" had outstayed its welcome. So, I became willing to let that role go.

Although, you would think letting go would mean giving up power and self, the opposite held true. By choosing to let go I gained the freedom to choose something different rather than remaining in victim mode. Choosing opened up the window of opportunity and the door of possibility and allowed life to flow through once again.

I'm not typically a skeptic; I usually consider myself a pretty hopeful, open and willing type of person. However, even I began to wonder where this worksheet would take me. I'll admit, the cynic in me had some doubts, but the pain of staying the same outgrew the pain of change. So I prayed that this exercise would take me somewhere. To where, I wasn't sure—resolution, I hoped. So I kept on going.

Had I given up at that point, I would have missed *it.*

**Mirror, Mirror, on the Wall...Who Reflects Me Most of All?**

While completing the worksheet's next section (questions eight to 10), the "Ah ha!" moment for which I was waiting arrived.

Question eight asked me to write down every judgment and expectation I ever had that related to my stepmom as well as every desire and way in which I wanted her to change. So I did. The bitterness I felt for her still left a foul taste in my mouth. I blamed her for a lot of things. Ok, everything. My words expressed a harshness of pure judgment and expectations set to my own standards. I just expected her to know and be these things, as if they came naturally for everyone. The usage of "shoulds" and "should nots" dominated my page, along with an obvious lack of acceptance.

Then I read Question #9:

**I am willing to realize that I get upset only when someone resonates in me those parts of me I have disowned, denied, repressed, and then projected onto them.**

"What? Run that by me again?" I thought. I reread the statement. Then, I looked at my list of emotions and thoughts about my stepmother one more time, delved a little deeper, and sure enough, plain as day, I had to admit the truth of the statement on that worksheet. Everything I had written about her actually could just as easily be written about me. Every line constituted a mirror. All those things I judged about her, expected from her, or in some way wanted to change about her, directly spoke like a message for me.

By this point I was stunned. My eyes glazed over like a deer in the headlights. If I hadn't taken the extra time to delve deeper into the "why," I wouldn't have realized that all the feelings and hurts I had towards my stepmom were really what I though about myself and projected onto her. She, in turn, simply reflected those thoughts back to me.

*This* was my breakthrough, and I felt as though I had been hit with a two by four right smack between the eyes. This pulling apart and tearing down of walls created the possibility for me now to change my perception and to move forward. I could once again look at the same set of circumstances with a new set of eyes, and, thus, forgave my stepmother. More importantly, I forgave myself.

This brought me to my next big question: How much of this, if any, is real?

Did any lack of love and understanding *really* exist in my father's home as I perceived? Did any abandonment really take place? What *really* happened? How much of my story was "story," and how much was based in actual fact? How much was created by a scared kid who couldn't make sense of what was happening or why? Would I ever know? Does it even matter anymore?

A new awareness and a slew of new questions poured out of me. Whatever I thought I knew, I really didn't—nor did it matter. However, with my new willingness to see something different paired with my new understanding, I saw my stepmom in a different light. I could see that she actually played quite a vital role in my life. By forgiving her, I healed myself and recreated my own, new reality. I had no more need for judgment and blame.

The book, *Radical Forgiveness,* suggests that our relationships consist of a series of spiritual contracts, agreed upon at the soul level, one that we carry out here on Earth with and for each other in order that we grow and learn as spiritual beings. If this is true, I realized my stepmother had one hell of a tough role to play in providing me with the the opportunity to learn what I needed to learn. Keeping this idea in mind, when I looked at her now I no longer saw the same "monster." This new picture reflected something much different—a gentler, softer person. I saw another human being doing the best she could every day…just like me. But I also saw a soul who loved me enough to give me the experience I wanted for my soul's journey, and for that I am now truly grateful.

"So, this is what peace feels like," I thought to myself.

117

In that moment, I understood the truth for the first time. I had caused my own misery. I had been a prisoner in my own prison, holding the keys to my own cell; I served as both captive and captor. How I thought about anything affected everything. Through the context of my hearing and listening to others, I gathered evidence to prove my thoughts about myself correct, and I made others wrong in the process. All my listening filtered through my belief that I was "not good enough," which lead to my state of low self-esteem and low self-confidence. It's amazing to think at some point in life "I" chose to believe that. What a rude, yet paradoxically wonderful, awakening. "I chose"—those two words possess a lot of power. Knowing this makes you think about using your words more wisely perhaps.

After completing this worksheet, almost instantly all the emotional baggage I had been carrying for the past 11 years vanished. Free from the story onto which I had clung so tightly and righteously, it no longer had power over me. I had gained my life back, and I currently continue to work at rebuilding it one baby step at a time.

One worksheet was all it took, but I didn't stop there. I printed off another. I took the same principles and used them with my father. I now enjoy a more peaceful relationship with him. I actually want to talk to him and have started rebuilding our relationship and regaining trust. Suddenly, "I love you" is not so hard to say to him.

**The Forgiveness Process Continues**

Forgiving my parents was the farthest thing from my mind for many long years. "You'll thank me someday," were the words I remember my father saying as I left his house, and I scoffed at them at the time. "No way in hell," I thought then. "After what I went through? What a joke. Keep dreaming."

He was right though, although not in the sense he thought. Today, I am truly grateful. I get it. In actuality, the whole experience turned out as a win-win. My father received his daughter back, and I received the greatest gift imaginable: the gift of self—self forgiveness, self love and self compassion. Despite how unconscious his statement was at the time and how much anger I felt, he was right. I *am* thankful, and I *do* thank him. And you know what? I love and appreciate him more now than I ever have.

If I regretted anything, it would be having wasted so many precious years hating those I actually love the most. I lived in resentment and slowly drank my own poison. Yet to regret means to waste a lesson learned and keeps me stuck in the past - so I don't. I take from my life experiences a powerful lesson that I would never have understood had it not unfolded *exactly* as it did. Everything happened perfectly in its own way. I trust that and surrender to it, and life becomes much easier. To not do so feels like I'm pushing a boulder uphill when the sign clearly states, "Other way."

My relationships with both my father and step-mother remain works in progress and are still by no means perfect. Every moment becomes a new learning and growing opportunity, a chance for a clean slate to make something anew. Power abounds in every choice.

While I once reserved "clean slate" as a term used in my travels, now it takes on more meaning and includes, "What do I want to create for myself" and "What matters most?" Inner peace and closure come to mind as do a talk with my parents, taking ownership, asking for forgiveness, and sincere gratitude for what it is they did give.

I continue to use the forgiveness worksheets to monitor myself, keep my reality in check, and deepen my understanding of my human self and my own soul's journey. This helps me see the truth behind my perceptions. Each unveiled moment, as inspiring as the next, is like a gift providing an opportunity to see the self and peel away the layers of untruth, so I can emerge through the fog of illusion. For this I give thanks. What started off as an opportunity to forgive others, turned out to be of far greater value: an opportunity for forgiveness of self. True to the adage, "What you sow, so shall you reap." With my new found awareness of how to separate fact from fiction combined with the power of choice, my ability to come from a place of love and appreciation, compassion and understanding, greatly increased, too.

Until the time I learned Radical Forgiveness, I didn't know that "my" truth was not necessarily "the" truth. Truth, as I discovered, merely represents a perception unique to the individual thinking it. As my perception changed, so did my life. From this place of empowerment, I make every day a Radical Forgiveness day and a chance to reframe and redefine my reality. As I do so, I give myself and those I love a tremendous gift: forgiveness. Forgiveness truly is the gift for-*giving*.

# 6. Healing At Work

The Company President Forgives His Father and his
Grandfather and Saves the Company

## By Colin Tipping

**Note:** *This story was first published in my book, 'Spiritual Intelligence at Work.' I wrote the story to illustrate how a childhood wound can be carried throughout life and remains likely to become acted out periodically as a way to heal itself. I have included it is in this book since it does show quite dramatically how this process, if not understood and provided for with Radical Forgiveness, can be very detrimental to the person, his or her family and, in this case, his company. The story is entirely fictional.*

### BOB

It was Bob's fiftieth birthday. Nevertheless, he was making his way to the office at his normal hour. He liked to be at his desk by 6:45 a.m. every day, which meant departing from home at around 6:15, leaving Jean and the two kids still fast asleep.

That way he could avoid the morning traffic and get a decent amount of work done before the general hubbub of the working day began with all its demands, pressures and distractions. Also, being something of a loner, he liked to have at least some part of the day to himself.

As usual Mrs. Harper, his secretary, arrived on time at 8:30 a.m. She was the only one who knew that it was his birthday. Bob had told her explicitly that he did not want a party or anything like that. Neither did he want anyone else to know that it was his birthday — especially his fiftieth. He didn't feel like celebrating anything, so he'd much rather it went unnoticed.

Bob was a little below average height with a slim athletic build. His hair was mostly thick and dark except for graying temples. You might not, at first glance, take him for fifty. Where he really did show his age, though, was around the eyes. Deeply set and ice blue, they were not at all easy to see beneath his bushy eyebrows, which were knitted into a perpetual frown — obviously the result of many years of stress and worry. His finely chiseled face and open smile made up for it though. He was really quite handsome.

Still, he was not feeling good about reaching fifty and didn't want attention brought to the fact. He just wanted the day to pass unnoticed, and to be like any other ordinary day. In fact, Bob was feeling more depressed than normal and didn't really know why. For the last six months he had been feeling very disturbed; as if something were gnawing at him from the inside.

He'd had similar experiences in the past but had always managed to push the feelings away by immersing himself in his work. As president of the company he always had a mountain of work that he never could get the better of, so it had always been easy for him to bury those feelings by working long hours.

This time it didn't seem to be working. Lately he was finding himself unable to really focus on his work, becoming indecisive and reclusive. He was biting people's heads off and being demanding, critical and really hard on the very people on whom he depended.

Throughout the company people were talking about the situation, and many of them were beginning to wonder whether their boss was really up to the job. It wasn't just affecting the senior management team who had to deal with him every day, but was trickling down the ranks and affecting morale throughout the firm.

In a company employing around fifty people there is still a possibility of there being something akin to a family atmosphere, especially when, as was the case with GiCo Inc., many of the employees had been there for several years, having been promoted up through the ranks. In GiCo's case, this had produced a loyalty and a synergy that had worked really well over the years. But, as with any extended family, if one part becomes dysfunctional, everyone senses it and a major disturbance results.

One such disturbance had occurred five years earlier when the man who had been president of the company for the last thirty-five years retired. Contrary to expectations, the board appointed someone from outside the company. That person was, of course, Bob Pearson.

There were at least two people at GiCo who had coveted that job for many years, both of whom probably would have accepted the appointment of the other with equanimity. So when an outsider was appointed, the two contenders were both flabbergasted and enraged. They felt totally betrayed. One of them took early retirement and left. He died within the year.

Bob's appointment also split the company, since those loyal to the contenders were openly hostile to Bob and were uncooperative for at least the first two years. In many parts of the company the wound still festered, even after five years.

Dennis Barker, the other contender for the job that Bob landed, did not leave the company. As vice president of sales and marketing he was, in effect, Bob's number two; but it was clear that he considered himself superior to Bob, both in intellect and experience.

Dennis made an effort to be a good number two, but it actually wasn't in him to be satisfied with that position. He always wanted to be number one. Bob could sense the resentment that was just beneath the surface, and Dennis would covertly act it out. He would find ways to withhold important information from Bob or to subtly undermine him in the minds of the management team.

The sabotage was never overt enough for Bob to challenge him on it, for Dennis was too clever to leave himself open to that. But the passive-aggressive behavior was always there. He also never lost an opportunity to finesse Bob in a way that confirmed for himself — and for Bob too, probably — his superiority.

Dennis was physically overpowering as well. He weighed at least a hundred pounds more than Bob, and at six feet three inches, he towered over Bob, who was only five feet eight inches tall. Whereas Bob moved quickly and easily, Dennis was lumbering and slow by comparison; he also had a slight stoop.

Even though Bob never let it show, he despised Dennis. He couldn't stand Dennis' false servility and insatiable need for approval. He felt Dennis was inauthentic and untrustworthy and saw him as the stereotypical sales type — great on the surface but with little substance beneath. He saw Dennis as manipulative, self-centered and needy.

Bob did pretty well in disguising these feelings, and to an outside eye, their relationship might seem cordial and even mutually respectful. But those who worked closely with the two of them knew better. They could feel the energy between them, and it was not good. Though the situation drained energy from the team, no one mentioned it — at least not openly and certainly not to Bob or Dennis.

## Meg

Meg saw her nine year-old daughter Caroline onto the school bus at 7:15 a.m. as she normally did, and then got back into the old Honda Civic she had managed to buy from her brother a couple of months before at a really good price. He had upgraded to a new SUV upon getting promoted at work. Knowing that Meg was struggling to make it as a single parent with no child support coming from her ex-husband, he let her have the car on a monthly payment basis. She made the drive to work in about 40 minutes and arrived ready to start work at 8:00 a.m.

Meg, having started in the shipping department, had been with GiCo for almost 8 years and in that time had progressed up the ladder to become a production supervisor. She was well thought of by those she supervised and, with the exception of one person, by everyone else in the company.

The exception was Monty Fisk, the production manager. For some reason he had it in for Meg and, as her boss, was making her life miserable. Everything had been fine for the first three years. He would sing her praises and give her all the resources she needed.

Then suddenly, after she had been there three years, everything switched. From that point on nothing was ever right, not only with her but with all those she supervised. He found fault with them all at every opportunity. Meg frequently ended up having to defend her staff members against him. They loved her for it, but it put a lot of stress on her and only made her relationship with Monty worse.

He took every opportunity to load her up with additional responsibilities and then set her up to make mistakes so he could find fault with her. Every time an opportunity came up for a possible promotion for Meg, he blocked it. And he would do it in a very perverse way. He knew that she was popular and well thought of, so he couldn't openly bad-mouth her.

His strategy was to say that she was so good at what she did and was now carrying so much responsibility that she was indispensable. He would claim that to move her would be extremely detrimental to the department. Somehow, he always managed to convince the executive management that Meg should be neither promoted nor moved sideways out of Monty's reach, something she had tried on a number of occasions to achieve.

On this particular morning she walked into her department to find people huddled around a certain young woman who was crying. "What's going on?" asked Meg.

"Mr. Fisk really chewed her out in a very nasty way over something that was not her fault and has threatened to put her on performance probation," replied one of Meg's team members. "That man is a pig!"

As Meg garnered as much detail as she could about the exchange, she felt the rage building up inside. "Why is this man making life so difficult for my staff and me?" she thought. "It's not fair and I have to put a stop to it now!"

She stormed into Monty's office. He was waiting for her, leaning way back in his chair, hands clasped behind his head and feet up on the desk, looking triumphant.

She slammed the door behind her and stood there fuming, looking at him with eyes ablaze. She was tall, slim, and very attractive, but right then she looked quite capable of killing someone — in this case, Monty Fisk.

"Why did you do that to her?" she shouted at him. "You know how she is — how easily upset she can get, and what you accused her of was not legitimate anyway, and you know it. Why do you have to be such a bully?"

He slowly took his feet off the desk, lowered his large bony hands and stood up. He was a tall, powerfully built man, and he pulled himself up to his full height. His eyes were cold and piercing. "Sit down!" he commanded in a quiet but menacing voice.

She remained standing, breathing heavily, defiant but scared. "Sit down!" he repeated, this time with a good deal more volume. She sank down into the chair. He remained standing with both hands on the desk leaning over towards her and looking down at her.

"Let me tell you something, Meg," he said quietly. "I know you think you are *Little Miss Popular* around here but I have the measure of you. You came into this company, and you advanced quickly. Do you know why?"

Not waiting for a reply, he went on. "What you don't know is that you only got your promotions because I made them happen. I saw your ability early, and I wanted to have you working for me, so I went out of my way to have you pro-moted. You have your job for one reason only — be-cause of me. And I can undo what I have done if I have a mind to. I have a lot of clout in this company, Meg, be-cause I get things done and I help them make a lot of money. I've been here a long time, and at this level what I say goes. Understand?"

Meg just sat there, saying nothing yet feeling an intense hatred for this man. He was intimidating her, but she held his gaze. There was a long pause before Monty spoke. "You did real well for a time, and I was pleased with the way you worked. To a large extent, Meg, I still am and I wouldn't want to lose you. But you've become too damn cocky, and you constantly try to undermine my authority," continued Monty. "And I won't let you. Do you hear me? I know how you speak to the people out on the shop floor about me, and I notice how you build yourself up to be the Mother Superior around this place. I am in charge around here, Meg, not you!

"Your are here to do my bidding and to do it the way I tell you to do it. I am tired of you making up your own rules and doing things any way you want. From this point on, you'd better do things the way I say they are to be done, or I might suggest to those in power some changes that you might not like. Do I make myself clear, Meg?"

"Quite clear." said Meg.

"That's good. Now get out there and get back to your job!" said Monty.


### Bob

Bob Pearson was no fool. He was aware that he was slipping, and it made him very fearful. He was seeing a recurring pattern, and he didn't like it.

When an executive search firm had recruited him away from HEH, Inc., he knew it had been timely. While during the first three years of his tenure as president of that company he had produced substantial growth for it, the results had been a lot weaker during the last two and were showing a pattern of steady decline. Relationships had deteriorated, and he'd begun to feel he might be losing his touch. He appeared to be sabotaging himself in many instances and was making a lot of poor decisions. He wasn't happy there.

So when the search firm had called and suggested this position at The Gyroscopic Instrument Company (GiCo), he had jumped at it. The salary was comparable, so he didn't feel demoted, plus they offered some very rich benefits. Thinking that perhaps a smaller company would better suit his management style, Bob had welcomed the opportunity.

"Happy birthday, Mr. Pearson." said Mrs. Harper in a low voice while slipping an envelope containing a very tasteful birthday card onto his desk. "Per your request, I haven't broadcast the fact of your reaching half a century — though I have to say that you don't look your age — and I don't think anyone else has remembered. You never have been one to make a fuss on your birthday, so nobody thinks much about it. Oh! Look here! Someone else does, though."

She was referring to an e-mail that had come through that morning. Bob usually checked e-mails himself during his early morning routine, but he had been so introspective on this particular day, he hadn't done so.

"Somebody from your old firm. Here." She passed him the printout and quickly busied herself so as to avoid any eye contact with her boss.

The e-mail was from Rick Tanner, his old business partner from way back. Bob and Rick had started a marketing business together twenty-five years ago.

As with Bob's later ventures, all had gone well for about three years, and then things started to go south. The business almost went bankrupt, but someone decided to invest in the company and rescue it — but only on the condition that Bob leave. Rick had been the negotiator, and Bob always felt that Rick had engineered his departure.

It had been a huge blow to Bob, and for a long while he struggled to get back on his feet. But he did so eventually and found himself a good position as marketing manager of another firm that, through no fault of his own, subsequently went out of business. He then joined HEH, Inc., an engineering firm, as marketing director and subsequently, became president.

He and Rick were the same age, and although they hadn't been in contact for many years since the breakup, it was apparently the fact of it being their fiftieth that had prompted the e-mail.

> *Happy Birthday, Bob.*
> *We've both made half a century.*
> *Congratulations are in order, I think.*
> *Call me and let's catch up.*
>
> *Rick.*

## Meg

Meg returned to her department seething with rage but feeling powerless. Monty had made it quite clear that he had the power to make things very difficult for her and perhaps even to get her fired. He had the authority to make that happen. Meg knew that.

131

By this time, the worker whom Monty had admonished was back at her station feeling sure that Meg had done all she could on her behalf to put things right with the manager. But Meg knew different. She had made no headway at all, and she felt as though she had let the woman down. She felt like giving notice right away.

"Why should I stay and be treated like dirt," she thought, "just because he feels so insecure and threatened by my efficiency and my ability to get the best out of people?"

This was true about Meg. She certainly had the physical bearing and presence of someone who could command respect; but she also showed a flexibility of approach that enabled the people she supervised to really trust her. This combination of strength and softness did indeed enable her to get productivity out of people in a way that Monty Fisk could never do.

But she quickly realized that leaving GiCo was out of the question. That's why she hadn't stood up to Monty. She knew she couldn't leave this company, especially now. Her husband had left her a year ago after four years of marriage, disappearing completely and leaving a lot of debt. He had become very violent and abusive, so she wasn't sorry to see him go; but there was no child support, no weekend visitations to give her a break, nothing.

She was completely on her own. Her parents were both dead, and all her brothers and sisters lived in other states. She was trapped, and she knew it.

There was another factor too that was preying on her mind. Even though she was only thirty-five, she knew that her health was not good. She'd had a couple of bouts of chronic fatigue syndrome in the past, and she was sensing that it might be returning. Lately, she was finding herself feeling very low on energy and needing more than a normal amount of sleep.

On the two previous occasions, she had just managed to cope well enough for people not to notice. Fortunately it had not been very severe, but to Meg, who was a single parent working at a stressful job, it had seemed debilitating. During those times she found it necessary to sleep virtually almost every hour that she wasn't working or taking care of the home and Caroline.

By doing that, she conserved enough energy to be able to effectively do her job, but by the end of the day she was truly exhausted. Each bout lasted about two months. She had researched the literature on CFS and was very aware that it can become extremely debilitating, so she knew she couldn't afford to lose her health insurance.

Meg had not had an easy life. She came from a pretty dysfunctional family. Her father was an alcoholic, and her mother was obsessive-compulsive and ultra critical. Everything had to be perfect for her, which meant that whatever Meg did was never good enough.

However hard she tried to please her mother, she could never win her approval. Meg's mother blamed her for everything and, perhaps because Meg was the eldest child, used her as the scapegoat for all the dysfunction within the family. Meg's father was in and out of work because of his drinking and he began molesting her when she was three years old. As it is for many girls who are molested by their fathers, she initially found it pleasurable and enjoyed getting the attention from the man she had put on a pedestal and from whom she got no attention at all except in that way.

At the same time, however, the deep knowing that it was wrong and shouldn't be happening would well up inside her and induce terrible guilt and fear. The longer the molestation went on, the worse Meg's feelings became. She was extremely frightened of him, and although she wanted the abuse to stop, she was powerless to do anything about it.

She did what most abuse victims do in this situation: she split herself off and disassociated from what was happening and then repressed the pain. When she was twelve, she tried to tell her mother about the abuse but her mother only became extremely enraged about it and would not listen. She just denied it and then shamed Meg even more for suggesting such a thing. Meg felt totally trapped and abandoned.

Finally, at age sixteen, Meg left home. She basically ran away without telling her parents where she was going, which was no big deal since they were too out of it to care anyway. For the next few years she became very promiscuous and totally irresponsible. She tried being in a lesbian relationship for a while, but that didn't work out.

At age twenty-four she was badly beaten and raped by a man she met in a bar one night. That incident put her into the hospital for three days, but fortunately, she recognized it as her wake-up call. She decided then to give up drinking and drugs and to really pull her life together. She moved, got a decent job, and began building her life again. She got married at twenty-five to a man who had seemed decent enough at first, but who very soon became violent and emotionally abusive. He drank heavily, and Meg often feared for her life when he would come home drunk.

Her daughter Caroline was from this marriage, but there was doubt about who the father was because Meg had had a short but passionate affair with another man. Her husband never suspected, but Meg became fearful for Caroline's safety as well as her own, so she eventually left that marriage and was divorced at twenty-eight.

She did well on her own for a while but she was lonely and in need of support. The chronic fatigue happened during this time, and it scared her to think that she might not be able to support herself and Caroline. She got married again, mostly for that reason, this time to a man who wasn't exactly abusive but who became emotionally unavailable very soon after the wedding.

It was a relationship without passion or interest. It was just dull. Meg wasn't the sort of woman to put up with that so she left him. At thirty-four she found herself alone once more.

Having come out of two failed marriages, Meg pretty much made up her mind that she wasn't going to marry, or even live with a man again, at least not until Caroline was grown up and gone. "All men are selfish and irresponsible," she would say. "They just use you and dump you, and I just don't want anything to do with any of them! I'm fine on my own."

In the year since she had become divorced, she had indeed done pretty well on her own. She had more or less gotten herself out of debt and managed to keep the mortgage paid, keep a car, and take care of herself and Caroline. She had progressed in the company and was earning a decent wage. It seemed that the only fly in the ointment was Monty. "Why does he have to make things so difficult for me?" she wondered.

As she sat there in her office thinking about it and still fuming, she wondered aloud how she could get back at him. "Get him fired perhaps? Now wouldn't that be good? Well, no. Can't do that. But I'll make sure he gets no cooperation from me in the future. I'm tired of working hard and making him look good."

The bell indicating that it was time for her department to take a coffee break shook her out of her obsessive thinking about how to get back at Monty. "Gotta get on with the job," she told herself. "But let me get a good strong cup of coffee first!"

## Bob

The e-mail had unsettled Bob even more than he already had been before Mrs. Harper had handed it to him. "Why would he write after all these years? Our relationship ended so acrimoniously."

Mrs. Harper was still in earshot but he was really talking to himself. She chose not to respond. Bob felt some pain in the area of his heart and knew it instinctively to be a reminder of the pain of being in that relationship — the pain that he had largely suppressed.

Right from the start Rick had made him feel "less than." No matter how hard he worked or how much effort he put in, it was never enough. Rick found fault with everything he did. Even though they were, in fact, equal partners, Rick always acted as if he were the boss and had treated Bob accordingly, often making decisions unilaterally.

Where Bob was cautious and conservative, Rick was a risk taker. It was this quality that had gotten the company into financial trouble and headed towards bankruptcy. He managed to twist everything around and made it look as if it were all Bob's fault, pointing to Bob's "weak management style" as the cause of the failure. Rick succeeded to the extent that the investors who came in to rescue the company agreed with him and made it a condition of the bailout that Bob had to go.

It had been a huge betrayal for Bob. It hadn't helped Bob's self esteem either to learn that, after he left, the company leaped ahead and then years later went public. Rick virtually retired a multimillionaire at age forty-two.

Bob looked again at the e-mail and decided not to take Rick up on the suggestion that they reconnect. The memory of it all was just too much. He crumpled the e-mail very tightly into a ball and tossed it into the trash can. The pain in his chest did not go away.

Mrs. Harper noticed the pained expression on Bob's face but decided to say nothing nor even to let him know that she noticed. She had been working for him for the entire time he had been at the company but had recently found herself having to tiptoe around him all the time, making sure not to get him upset. The president of the company was clearly not himself.

## Monty

Monty was fuming and breathing heavily. It took him quite some time to compose himself after Meg turned her back and walked out of his office, slamming the door hard as she left.

There was something about Meg he just couldn't abide. It seemed that hardly a day passed by where she didn't find some way to get under his skin. Everything she did seemed to upset him — and often to a disproportionate extent. He frequently had to admit that to himself.

He also had to concede that she was a good worker who did her job well — there was no doubt about that. The workers adored and respected her because she was both firm and fair. They didn't mess with her, but whenever the need arose, she stood up for them — oftentimes against him. That really angered him.

When she had first joined the company and begun working for him, he had been very comfortable with her. He found her to be teachable and responsive, intelligent and willing to grow into the job. He had liked Meg in the beginning and had vigorously supported her promotion to production supervisor. But as she came into her power and began to exercise more and more responsibility, Monty's feelings began to change. He felt threatened by her. He began to feel that she was undermining him at every opportunity and setting the workers against him. He felt defensive around her, and although she always treated him with due respect, he felt dominated by her in some strange way. She seemed so overpowering!

Monty sat there at his desk, going over what had just happened, feeling puzzled and perplexed. He never thought of himself as an angry man. So why so much anger? What was it about Meg that upset him so much? He couldn't figure it out at all, other than to assume it was some kind of personality clash. He had to admit that he had chewed that worker out on purpose, knowing that Meg would rise to the bait and come in with guns ablaze, giving him the opportunity to put her down. But he still couldn't quite understand why he needed to do it.

Whatever the reason, Monty resolved to stay on top of her and not let her get the better of him. She had so much support from the workers that she could easily usurp his authority and become, in effect, the boss. He must not allow that to happen.

"I need to clip her wings," he said to himself, thinking that it wasn't beyond the bounds of possibility that Meg might threaten his position in the company by causing labor disputes over his leadership style.

"That won't happen," he said as if to comfort himself. "Bob Pearson will support me over her any day." With that he returned to work.

There did, in fact, exist an unusually close bond between the president and his production manager, such that Monty had every reason to feel more secure in his job than he otherwise might. They had met when they both worked at the company Bob joined after being ejected from his own company by Rick. Bob was a few years older than Monty but saw a great deal of potential in him. Monty was talented, sharp and had a natural flair for organization and production.

While Bob had actually been on the sales and marketing side of that business, he really felt a greater affinity to the manufacturing and production side. In that sense, he was a square peg in a round hole. That being so, he began to derive a vicarious satisfaction from mentoring Monty. Bob used what influence he had at the time to make sure that Monty had ample opportunity to grow in the company during the five years Bob was there.

When Monty eventually applied for and landed another job, Bob felt not only disappointment but a strong sense of betrayal. Monty had not even mentioned he was looking for another position. Bob knew his feelings were irrational and that he had no right to expect Monty to stay. Nothing was ever said, but Monty felt Bob's disappointment and anger.

He did stay in touch with Bob, if only sporadically and mostly by e-mail. Usually it was just to share some success at work, a promotion perhaps and the contact occurred no more than a couple of times a year.

However, when Monty heard that the president of the company where he worked, GiCo, Inc., was retiring and that the likelihood was that either one of two people he despised equally in the company were likely to take his place, he immediately thought of his old mentor, Bob Pearson, who was at that time president of HEH, Inc.

Having Bob at the helm of the company where he worked would secure his own position nicely, Monty had reasoned. Monty would do anything to stop Dennis Barker from becoming president. He'd frequently had run-ins with Dennis and knew that if Dennis became president, life might become very precarious.

Dennis Barker was always bitching about how the production department did not keep the sales force properly supported, but as far as Monty was concerned it was Dennis Barker's inefficiency and inability to plan ahead that caused the problems. Dennis treated him with disdain, and Monty could barely bring himself to talk with Dennis.

Monty had dashed off an e-mail letting Bob know that a search firm had been given the task of finding a new president for GiCo. He gave Bob a contact number he had somehow acquired and left it at that. Bob took the bait, and the rest was history.

The debt had only once been acknowledged and, even then, well before Bob took the helm at GiCo. From the moment Bob arrived at the firm, Monty had been assiduous in maintaining a careful and respectful distance and had never tried to curry favor with Bob. Neither had Bob resumed his mentoring role, and he treated Monty just like any of his other managers.

However, Monty always knew that he had an ace in the hole and that, one day, he might need to make use of it. It gave him a lot of comfort.

## Dennis

Whenever Dennis Barker entered the room, it was like someone had opened the door and allowed a gust of wind to blow in and completely occupy the space. His energy was enormous, and he got your attention immediately, and yet there was always something inauthentic about him. One never could feel quite comfortable with him. He was always too eager to please and generous to a fault; people always felt there was another agenda behind everything Dennis said and did. "I've got the figures, Bob." he said as he blew into the room.

"How do they look?" asked Bob with a sinking feeling. He knew they weren't going to be good.

"Not so great," replied Dennis. "We need to talk. Is this a good time? I can come back later if you like."

Bob motioned with his hand for Dennis to sit and held out his hand for the most recent sales figures that Dennis had just prepared. Dennis sat down and drew his chair up closer to Bob's desk. "Oh, and by the way, happy birthday," he said.

Bob peered over his spectacles at Dennis and just grunted, nodding in reluctant acknowledgment. He felt anything but happy. Dennis cast a glance back and gave a shrug as if to say, "Well, I tried."

He knew Bob was depressed and struggling to stay together for some reason. Dennis had no idea what was eating Bob but surmised that he and Jean might be having troubles at home. She seemed nice enough, but she liked all the trappings and was always out spending Bob's money at all the finest stores. Perhaps she had gotten him into serious debt. Dennis doubted it though. It seemed Bob was troubled more by what was inside him than by any external circumstances.

Dennis had been watching Bob like a hawk over the last six months and was very aware that Bob was not himself and might even be losing his grip. This might be his chance to replace Bob, he allowed himself to think, but he would need to play his cards very carefully.

"This is just a temporary dip in the figures, Bob," Dennis said reassuringly. "They'll pick up next quarter for sure. We had so many things not going for us this quarter that will not be factored in next time around. The sales team is much stronger now, and we have built in some good incentives to improve performance."

"With the economy the way it is, we ought to be performing better than this, though," replied Bob as he looked over the figures.

"Bob, you must give yourself credit. Under your leadership, we doubled our net income for each of the first three years of your tenure. That was a tremendous achievement, and I have no doubt in my mind that no one else could have done it *(unspoken subtext: except me, of course)*. I agree it has slowed down somewhat, but it is still good and we are still growing. However, and I hate to

143

say this Bob, but if we have a problem at all, it is not with sales and marketing but with production."

Bob bristled. Manufacturing and production were his responsibility, and here was Dennis interfering again in his usual manner. He always came on first with the compliments and then hit you from behind with the criticism. Bob immediately snapped back at Dennis, "What are you saying?"

Dennis knew he was on dangerous ground and would have to tread carefully, but he had seen an opportunity. "We need to modernize our systems, Bob. Our costs are much higher than our competitors', and yet we still have to compete on price and service. The sales people are very frustrated because we are consistently unable to supply the product in a timely fashion and they lose sales as a result of that."

"I'm ahead of you on this, Dennis," replied Bob. "I have already asked Monty Fisk to submit ideas for modernizing the plant."

Dennis leaned forward in his seat, not looking at Bob but at his own feet with his hands tightly clasped together between his legs. He knew how to use his energy to create presence. Pausing for quite some time, he finally looked at Bob and said, "But Monty Fisk is the problem, Bob."

"What the hell do you mean?" Bob responded angrily. "Monty Fisk is a hell of a good production manager."

In his spare time Dennis was a fly fisherman and a good one at that. Now he felt almost as if he were playing Bob like a fish on a line. Bob had taken the bait and now Dennis had to carefully reel him in.

Though Bob didn't realize it, Dennis knew only too well that Monty Fisk had tipped him off about the opening for president and was, in that sense, at least partly responsible for Dennis not getting the job. He hated Fisk, so there was a score to settle there too — but of course Bob, or rather his job, was the bigger fish. He was using a 'minnow to catch a mackerel,' as they say, and it would be sweet revenge indeed if he could dispose of them both at the same time.

Not only did he know of their connection and the debt that Bob owed Monty, but in doing his homework well, Dennis had discovered that Bob had been Monty's mentor for some years prior. That added another whole dimension to the situation and further ammunition.

"He's of the old school, Bob," replied Dennis softly. "He won't modernize — he's too stuck in his ways. He doesn't understand computers and is unable to hold a vision big enough to spearhead the kind of improvements needed to support the kind of growth we need to have if we want to keep our market share. Our competitors are way ahead of us in terms of efficiency and profitability, Bob, and you know it. We've been putting off the modernizing plan for some time now, to the point where some drastic action is required."

"You might be surprised!" Bob countered. "He'll be reporting to me with his suggestions for modernization by the end of this month. As soon as we have them, we'll have a meeting to discuss them. Until then, the subject is closed! Now, if there's nothing else, Dennis, I need to get back to work."

Clearly, the meeting was at an end, but Dennis felt pleased with the limited outcome of this exchange and, with all due deference, gracefully made his exit.

Dennis was a patient man but he was also driven. He wanted Bob's job so much he could taste it. He had watched Bob build the company fast in his first three years but was now recognizing the signs that Bob was weakening. His patience and stealth were starting to pay off, and he was about to turn up the heat.

Over the past twelve months, Dennis had carefully sown seeds of discontent about Bob among the management team. This had trickled down to the shop floor and to the sales team. As a result, people were now beginning to question Bob's ability as president.

Using divide-and-rule tactics, Dennis nurtured the discontent between sales and marketing and the production departments, and put the squeeze on Monty Fisk so he would feel vulnerable. Dennis knew that in order to survive, Monty would play his ace card on Bob, which would create enormous embarrassment for Bob and perhaps even a crisis. That was exactly what Dennis wanted.

# BOB

Though he had escaped birthday celebrations at work, Bob was not to be let off so lightly at home. Jean had arranged a surprise birthday party for him. He arrived home earlier than usual and found that she had invited several friends as well as his now quite aged father.

As he walked through the door they all sang "Happy Birthday," and his children rushed up to him to give him their gifts. Jean kissed him lovingly.

She was younger than Bob by eight years and was an attractive, stylish woman with shoulder-length, ash-blonde hair which she usually wore down, but on this occasion she had put it up. She wore a low-cut, tight fitting white dress that revealed quite of lot of her shapely figure. Bob did his best to look pleased about the party and, once things settled down a bit, proceeded to pour champagne for a toast.

"To my loving husband on his fiftieth birthday," said Jean simply. Everyone clapped and cheered.

"Thanks, everyone: let's eat," Bob said, pointing to the lavish buffet that Jean had catered in. Once he had filled his plate, Bob reluctantly made his way over to his father.

In spite of having lost a leg in the Second World War and then later becoming crippled through a car accident when Bob was just a baby, Bob's father had reached the age of seventy-nine. Though confined to a wheelchair for most of his life, he had managed to outlive Bob's mother by fifteen years. He was an extremely angry and bitter man.

"Hi, Dad. How are you doing?" Bob asked dutifully.

"Terrible!" came the reply that Bob had fully expected. "The pain gets worse every year, and those stupid doctors at the VA Hospital couldn't give a damn. Not one of them! Useless bastards, all of 'em. But I don't give in, and I still work my ass off in spite of the pain. I don't quit you know; not like some people I know."

There was the first jab of the evening that Bob knew was inevitable and inescapable. There would be more.
"And how about you? Still at that firm — what's it called?"

"GiCo, Dad."

"Yes, that's it, GiCo. Heard from that old partner of yours lately, the one who became a millionaire? You screwed up there, didn't you, boy? Shouldn't have left. You might have been a millionaire by now too."

"I didn't exactly leave, Dad, and I'm not doing so bad anyway. Does this make me look poor?" asked Bob, pointing to the house and everything in it.

"No, but you're not a millionaire either, are you? That partner of yours is a multimillionaire, though, isn't he? Let's face it, Bobby, you both started out together as partners and you let him screw you over. Pity you're not more like your brother. Jimmy wouldn't have let that bastard squeeze him out. No siree! If it had been him and not you, I wouldn't have lost the money I put into that business to help you get going. Hard-earned cash — made by my own hands, let me tell you, even though I am in a damned wheelchair. I ended up losing my money because of you."

"Must you bring that up again, Dad? You know darn well I repaid that debt years ago."

"Yeah, so I got my money back, but I might have been a millionaire when Rick took that company public if you hadn't screwed up, just like I knew you would. Instead, I have to rely on my pension and whatever I make by selling my woodworking."

"Fuck you, Dad!" said Bob and moved away. He could feel the rage welling up in him, and he was close to tears. He hated the man and wished that Jean had not invited him. Even though his mother had not been emotionally available for him during his early years, he nevertheless missed her and wished all the time that it was his father that had died of cancer instead.

When Bob was a young boy, his father would always put him down and would frequently belittle him in front of people. "Look at him," he would shout and scream. "He'll never amount to anything; no damn use to anyone! Thank God his brother Jimmy isn't like him!"

As is typical with this kind of primal wounding, and in spite of all the shaming and the beatings that inevitably followed, Bob had unconsciously spent all his boyhood and most of his adult life trying to get his father's approval and never succeeding.

Every time Bob had experienced failure in his life, his thoughts would go straight to his father and the shame would be unbearable. Conversely, whenever he achieved success, no matter how good it was, he knew it would never be enough.

As a boy, Bob was athletic, wiry and strong. He was not one for team sports, but he was a good long-distance runner. He ran in a lot of races and won a fair number of trophies. His father never came to watch or support him, except once. That was when Bob was fourteen and was representing his high school in a ten-mile cross-country race. Bob came in first but only a few yards in front of the next contender. The only comment his father made was, "You nearly lost!"

The only person Bob had felt really loved him and made him feel worthwhile was his grandfather. He lived close by, and from a very early age, Bob spent as many hours with him as he could. Bob's mother and father took no notice of him anyway, so they didn't care. His grandfather had a little workshop and would show Bob how to do things with bits of wood and metal. With him, Bob did not feel alone.

Though he visited his grandfather most days, there was one day that Bob, for whatever reason, decided not to. That was the day his grandfather died. The neighbors had found him in his workshop, having died alone of a massive heart attack.

Bob was just five years of age, but it felt to him as if his whole world had come crashing down. He had lost the only person in the world that loved him and saw him for who he was. He had never felt so desperately alone, and yet, he could share none of his pain with his parents, least of all his father. His father had just told him not be so stupid. "Cryin' is for girls," he said and told Bob to stop crying or he would give him something to cry about.

Bob also blamed himself for the death. "If only I had gone there as usual, I might have been able to save him — or at least call an ambulance," he would always think to himself. Bob never got over the loss.

Fortunately, the guests left pretty early and, thank God, someone helped Bob's father get himself into the wheelchair-adapted mini-van that he drove. Bob had said nothing more to him the whole evening and was glad to see him go. He did not even say good-bye, and neither did his father.

"The mean old bastard," he said quietly to Jean as they watched him go. "I'll hate him until the day he dies, and then some."

"I'm sorry I invited him, Bob, but it felt right somehow that I should. It's been so long since you two have spoken, and after all, it is your fiftieth. But I know now that I shouldn't have. I'm sorry"

Bob turned and looked at his wife. She looked alluring in her low-cut dress, and whereas normally he would have been quick to seize the moment, he felt no desire for her tonight. "I've got to go to bed," he said. "I am so desperately tired." With that, and with his head held low, he went upstairs. Jean knew him well enough to know that something was desperately wrong, so for the first time in her life she left the house just as it was and immediately followed him upstairs to bed. She knew that he needed her.

Bob ended his fiftieth birthday in the arms of his wife, crying uncontrollably for most of the night. And he didn't know why.

## Meg

Meg couldn't get Monty off her mind. He had scared her that day — much more than she realized at the time. She really felt that he had it in for her, even though she did her job more or less perfectly.

She was a perfectionist about everything, but with Monty it counted for nothing. Whatever she did, it was not enough for him. Thank God that the workers cared for her and that she was able to put her energy into taking care of them.

Meg collected Caroline from school and went straight home. Immediately after cooking them both a light meal, she crashed.

## Mrs. Harper

Gwen Harper was one of those women who you might think had been born with energy-sensing antennae. She could not only register emotional tension between people three blocks away but would have a pretty good sense of what it might be about. Not that she was psychic. The kind of sensitivity she had came from being brought up in a house where one or both parents are not only alcoholic but violent rage-a-holics as well.

To survive and to stay out of trouble for as long as possible, Gwen had had to develop an ultra sensitive awareness of where the next emotional outburst might come from and to recognize the warning signs instantly.

She also learned to say very little or, better still, to say nothing about what she saw or heard going on around her. The safest strategy was to act as if nothing had happened and be as invisible as possible.

She continued to effect that strategy at GiCo, much as she had likely done in her own marriage. Her husband had died ten years ago, and her four children were all grown and married. She lived alone with her two cats.

Gwen was fully aware of all the ongoing tensions between Bob Pearson and Dennis Barker, and she saw through all the subtle and not-so-subtle power plays in which each of them indulged. But they didn't know that, of course. She had perfected the art of being invisible and giving the impression of being totally unaware of what was happening around her. She never spoke of what she observed and never offered advice. She had strong opinions, of course, but she always kept them to herself.

She also knew a lot about Bob Pearson's background by virtue of the fact that her old school friend, Barbara Fields, had ended up marrying Rick Tanner. Gwen had maintained that connection and had therefore, through Barbara, heard all about the drama that occurred when Rick forced Bob Pearson out of their partnership.

Naturally, she saw it all through Barbara Tanner's eyes at the time and never did meet Bob. Neither had she ever let on to Bob when he joined the firm that she was an acquaintance of the Tanners or that she knew what had happened. She almost lost it, though, when that e-mail came in from Rick on Bob's birthday. She came close to letting out a gasp when she saw it, but Bob was too self-absorbed to notice.

153

Her awareness of what was going on was not limited to the executive floor. She somehow managed to stay in tune with the emotional energy field of the entire firm. She had a good ear for the gossip that is common between secretaries and assistants, and she was able to make correct intuitive connections with only the smallest tidbits of information. She was also able to confirm her intuitions by going to the personnel files to which, as the president's personal assistant, she had unfettered access.

Gwen came from a large family. She was the second of six children: four boys and two girls. Her older brother, 3 years her senior, treated her just like her father treated her mother. Her father was of the firm opinion that women didn't matter much and didn't require a higher education because they would become either a nurse, a school-teacher, or a secretary.

When her father sold his business for 14.4 million dollars, the boys got equal shares; the two girls got nothing. Not a penny. Gwen was furious but could never confront her father. He was just too powerful, and she was terrified of him.

Her mother was a kind and sweet soul with a weak body. She was always sick in bed or moving around feeling terrible. It saddened Gwen to see her father be so demanding of her mother in spite of the fact that she was weak, exhausted and ill. It was as if he didn't even notice.

In order to protect her mother, Gwen began to work around the house at a very early age and to take care of the other children. Her only sister was the baby in the family, so basically Gwen became mother and maid in that household. The boys were not expected to help out in the house in any way, and her father expected to be looked after all the time.

Her early life was a real struggle, and when she got pregnant in her late teens, her father disowned her, saying she brought shame on the family even though she married the man prior to the child being born.

She despised Monty Fisk. She knew of his prior connection with Bob, of course, and understood only too well how he had set it up with the search firm to recruit Bob Pearson in order to sabotage Dennis Barker's chances of becoming president.

Not that Gwen Harper had much time for Dennis Barker either, let it be said, but she had been extremely attached and loyal to Charles Bottomly, the other candidate, who had died within a year of retiring. She really had wanted him to get the job, and she firmly believed that he would be alive today had he done so. In her mind, it was the disappointment that had killed him, and to a large extent, she blamed Monty Fisk.

It was also not escaping her keen attention that Dennis Barker was maneuvering himself to wrest back from Bob Pearson the job that Dennis had always felt was his, by aggravating and capitalizing upon Bob's current state of depression. She could read Dennis like a book.

Though she had been loyal to Charles Bottomly and was disappointed that Bob Pearson was appointed, she nevertheless liked Bob from the beginning. She very soon became willing to defend and protect him from all the covert negative energy that was projected towards him, and she wasn't going to stop now.

Neither was she going to let Dennis Barker hurt Bob. She was an extremely good and loyal secretary to Bob, but she was sensitive to his feelings too and worried about him when he felt down. It was all she could do not to mother him.

Besides having this uncanny ability to know everything that was going on without appearing to do so, and to remain more or less invisible, she also had a very strong caretaker streak. If she saw someone being treated unfairly in any way, she would feel their pain intensely and would work in very subtle ways to make sure that some restitution occurred.

In her mind, she saw the people who worked at GiCo as her family, and she felt a deep need to be responsible for them, just as she had been with her own siblings.

This need to be a "silent" caretaker and anonymous benefactor fitted in with her need to be invisible and to keep everything she knew inside and hidden. However, it led her to exist very much in her own inner world, separate from other people. Though on the surface she was quite sociable, no one could get close to her.

The shadow side of Gwen Harper's ability to "take care" of people without drawing attention to herself was that she was equally adept at secretly sabotaging those she didn't like and about whom she had strong judgments. She was very self-righteous and was always quite sure she knew what was best.

Her current concern, however, was with Meg Smith. She really liked Meg and felt very drawn to her, seeing a lot of herself in her perhaps. She had heard a lot about Meg and her wilder days but had developed a lot of respect for how Meg had pulled herself up by her bootstraps and made a decent life for herself when she might easily have gone the other way. Not that Gwen was above taking some credit for this herself. After all, it was she who had pulled a lot of strings to get Meg her job at GiCo.

It was during her abusive first marriage that Meg had met Rick Tanner and had a brief affair with him. His wife Barbara never knew about it, so Gwen, too, would have remained ignorant of that had Rick not called and asked if she could get Meg a job at GiCo.

He had said that she was a friend and just wanted to do her a favor, but Gwen could smell the guilt and the deception. She knew what a womanizer Rick was and knew immediately that he had, or was having, an affair with Meg. When Meg arrived at the interview, she was clearly pregnant, and even though Meg was married, Gwen had no doubt whatsoever in her own mind that the baby was Rick's.

At the time she was very angry with Meg for having the affair with her friend's husband and judged her severely, but she knew Rick well enough to know that it would have been mostly his fault. As time went by, she dropped her judgment and began to really like Meg. She saw a lot of herself there.

She recognized Meg as being a really good mother to Caroline and a very good supervisor at her work. She particularly appreciated the way that she took good care of her workers and was willing to defend them against that horrible tyrant and woman-hater, Monty Fisk.

She had been carefully tracking how Monty had turned on Meg and blocked her promotion on a number of occasions. Gwen had listened to Monty telling Bob Pearson how Meg needed strong handling and that she might be trouble if Bob moved her into another department and gave her a promotion. Bob always gave in to Monty, and Gwen Harper knew why, of course — which is why she decided that she would intervene as soon as the opportunity presented itself.

### Bob

Gwen Harper took the call. "Mrs. Harper, this is Jean Pearson. Would you please tell everyone who needs to know that Mr. Pearson will not be in today? I think he might have picked up a bit of food poisoning at the party we threw for him last night — not real serious, I don't think — so he should be in tomorrow. Would you do that for me? Thanks. Bye."

Bob threw a glance at Jean and wondered whether he would indeed be able to pull himself together sufficiently to return to work in the morning. He had never called in sick in his life, and for him to take a day off was quite unusual and totally out of character. *(That fact had not been lost on Mrs. Harper, either.)* He looked, and felt, terrible.

Jean had gotten the kids off to school, and now they were alone. She had been worried about him for months, but he would never talk about his feelings and always brushed her aside whenever she asked him if he was worried about anything.

"What's going on, Bob?" she asked. "You've never cried like that for as long as I've known you. You were like a scared little boy last night in bed. You need to talk about it, Bob, or you'll crack up."

Bob just stared vacantly into the fireplace. He would not look at Jean. Finally he said, "I'm scared of losing it all, Jean. I feel that I am in quicksand, and I am being sucked down."

"By what, Bob?" Jean asked.

"I don't know."

"Are things getting really difficult at work again? Is that it? Is Dennis putting pressure on you?" Jean waited for a response that was long in coming.
"Yes, but that's not it. I've had work troubles like this before, and I can handle Dennis Barker. I know he wants my job, but I'm always one step ahead of him."

"Then what is it, Bob? Is it us?"

"No," said Bob quickly, looking up at her. "It's not our relationship. I love you, and we're fine."

Jean had run out of questions and could only look at him and observe how pathetic and childlike he seemed at this moment.

"I feel like I am dying," he said.

"What do you mean?" Jean cried.

"Oh, don't panic — it's not my health. I'm fine physically. No, I'm not going to die — I'm just saying that this feels like death to me."

With that, Bob buried his head in his hands and then, after a few moments, got up and hurried to their bedroom. She knew he needed to cry alone.


## Dennis

After Gwen Harper had called and told him that Bob Pearson was sick and wouldn't be in, Dennis allowed himself a wry smile. He knew that Bob was close to a breakdown and sensed that this might be his best opportunity yet to oust Bob and take over his job.

From an early age, Dennis had been driven to be number one. In his eyes, coming second was the same as losing, so winning was everything to him. With that kind of mind-set, the ends always justified the means, and Dennis had followed that path all his life. So long as he won in the end, he had no qualms about how he did it.

But he was as smart a man as he was ruthless. He was extremely patient, knowing how to bide his time and wait for the right moment to strike. He also had perfected the art of the act and always gave the impression of being everything that he was not.

He had studied and mastered Neuro-Linguistic Programming (NLP). This is a form of awake-hypnosis that was originally designed as a powerful healing modality for reprogramming the subconscious mind. However, because it was a form of hypnosis that was performed while the person was totally conscious, it could also be performed surreptitiously.

This made NLP very attractive to people who wanted to manipulate others at the subconscious level without their being aware of it. Salesmen, obviously, thought of it as a blessing and Dennis was no exception. He became extremely adept at using it to control others. It was largely through his ability to control and manipulate people without their knowing, and to be how he thought others wanted him to be, that he advanced his career in sales in general and at GiCo in particular.

Dennis was born into a family of Irish descent. Both sets of grandparents had immigrated during the potato famine of 1910 and had settled in Boston. Dennis' parents were very poor and his father was a drinker. Dennis was the fifth child of eight and always felt that he had to fight for mere survival. He had always felt deeply ashamed of his family and vowed that he wasn't going to end up like his father, a broken man. Out of all the children, he was the one who took himself off to night school with the sole aim of lifting himself out of the lifestyle he despised and to escape the family he was so terribly ashamed of. He was intelligent and a fast learner.

He had succeeded in becoming a well-educated engineer, but he soon was drawn towards the sales side of the business. His Irish charm and a gift for quick thinking and fast talking made him a natural for sales. He had joined GiCo, Inc., some ten years previously as a technical salesman and had steadily risen through the ranks to become vice president at the age of thirty-six.

From very early on, Dennis had set his sights on the top job and was extremely disappointed and angry when he didn't get it. Not that he showed it, of course. That wasn't his style. He appeared to take it in his stride and to support the board's choice, but inside he was seething. He vowed that he would do whatever he had to do to wrest that job, at the earliest opportunity, from whomever held it at the time. Dennis would not be happy until he was number one at GiCo, Inc.

But he was never one to attack directly. Dennis knew that if he was too overt in trying to unseat the president, that Bob would fight him very hard and might well fire him.

No, he knew that the best way to get Bob Pearson was through Monty Fisk. With Bob away at least for a day and probably more than that, this was a good time to sow some seeds and to begin unsettling Monty to the point where Monty might feel it necessary to play his survival card with Bob Pearson. Dennis picked up the phone and asked his secretary to put a call through to Monty Fisk.


### Gwen Harper

Gwen Harper was also sharp enough to see an opportunity when it presented itself. She put a call through to one of the secretarial staff in the production department she trusted well enough to know that it wouldn't get to Monty

Fisk's personal secretary, to the effect that Mrs. Harper would like to have a word with Meg Smith. A few minutes later, her phone rang.

"Hello, Mrs. Harper, this is Meg Smith from production. I was told that you wanted to speak with me."

"That's right, Meg," Gwen replied. "I would like a word with you if you have a moment. Actually, I would prefer that it be off the premises. Would you care to have lunch with me today?"

"Of course," said Meg. "That would be nice. I get my lunch break around one o'clock. Is that OK? "

Gwen told Meg to meet her at 1:15 at a particular restaurant and to not let anyone, especially Mr. Fisk, know that she was having lunch with Gwen Harper. Meg arrived on time, and as soon as they had ordered, Gwen opened the conversation.

"Meg, I've been noticing that you haven't been yourself lately. You look very tired and stressed out. I'm worried about you. What's going on?"

"Oh, nothing really," Meg replied, a little taken aback by Gwen's directness. She had been wondering all morning why Gwen had quite uncharacteristically suggested a lunchtime meeting. "I'm just a little tired trying to be a mom as well as a full-time career woman. But I'm fine, really."

"Is Mr. Fisk still coming down hard on you?" asked Gwen, thinking that she had to come to the point quickly. "I'm hearing on the grapevine that he is making things really tough for you. Is that right?"

163

Tears immediately began coming to Meg's eyes. She could feel Gwen's concern for her and immediately connected with her compassion. Even though she was an executive secretary, Gwen could just as easily be your mother in moments like this.

Meg dropped her guard and began to relate to Gwen all that had been going on between her and Monty and how it was wearing her down and undermining her self-esteem. She told Gwen how Monty had threatened her the day before and how he had wielded his power over her. She just couldn't understand why he hated her so much, especially since in the early days he had seemed to like her and had supported her.

For her part, Gwen was acutely aware that her own dislike for Monty Fisk and her desire to protect Meg from his overbearing behavior were becoming even more intense.

"Please don't say anything to Mr. Pearson, Mrs. Harper," Meg pleaded. "If this gets back to Monty, my life won't be worth living."

"Don't worry, Meg. I won't. But I won't let Monty get away with anything either. If he threatens you again, I want you to let me know. I cannot stand injustice, and even more so, I hate the idea of men trying to use their strength to overpower women. I won't let it happen to you, Meg." Meg felt relieved and cared for. It was a good feeling.

When Gwen Harper got back to the office, she checked messages and found none from the Pearsons. She thought it was strange, but took advantage of the time and the freedom to go into the personnel files. She was hoping she could find something on Monty Fisk that would weaken his hold over Bob Pearson.

She was in something of a quandary though, because she sensed that Dennis was also getting ready to pounce on Monty Fisk for reasons of his own. She knew he knew about Bob and Monty and had been waiting for an opportunity to expose the whole situation in order to embarrass Bob, so she was not anxious to provide him with any ammunition. Dennis could care less about Meg Smith.

Gwen thought long and hard and then made a fateful decision that would ultimately change the fortunes of GiCo, Inc. She called Rick Tanner and told him about Bob.

### Bob

Bob slept virtually all that day, all through the night and into the next morning. Jean was happy about that. She knew that nothing heals like an extended sleep, and she left him alone as much as she could, except to bring him water and some snack food which he hardly touched. She saw it as the direct result of stress and feared that it might have been a nervous breakdown. It did not, however, occur to her that it might be his dark night of the soul.

Bob, on the other hand, had a sense of it being just that, though he would never have used that language to describe it. Yes, stress was a factor, but what was happening to him was caused by something far more profound. Some part of himself was boiling up and wanting to surface, but he didn't understand what it was or how he should react. Bob was scared.

165

About mid-morning a FedEx packet arrived. Jean looked at it but didn't open it before taking it up to Bob, who was now sitting up and feeling a little better. He opened it and found that it contained a book. He looked to see who had sent it, but it had been dispatched by a bookstore addressed to Mr. Robert Pearson. There was no note, no invoice, nothing.

The title of the book intrigued him: *RADICAL Forgiveness: Making Room for the Miracle.* He had never heard of the author nor even any of those who had endorsed the book. Shrugging his shoulders, he put it down on his bedside cabinet and went back to sleep.

Once more, Jean left him alone but kept on wondering who had sent Bob that book — and why that one? Not that he didn't need a miracle right now! "He could really use one," she thought.

After lunch that day, she decided she must talk with Dennis Barker and Gwen Harper and give them some idea when Bob might be returning. She didn't want to say too much, but there was no hiding that something quite serious was happening.

She told them that Bob was suffering from nervous exhaustion and that she thought he needed to take at least a week off, if not two. On the other hand, he would probably be available for consultation from home in the next day or two.

She only talked to Mrs. Harper, but she knew that the message would get to everyone who needed to know. She went back up to Bob about two hours later just to check on him and found him sitting up and almost devouring the book. He seemed to have gotten some of his life back all of a sudden.

"Jean, whoever sent this book must have known something. It's really quite extraordinary, and even though it's not my normal way of thinking, it is striking chords in me left and right."

"What does it say?" asked Jean, marveling at how Bob had really perked up.

"Hard to explain really, but it is starting to ring some bells. I'm even beginning to see what might be happening to me," he said almost to himself. "Let me finish reading this chapter, and then, rather than trying to explain it, I'll let you read the first chapter. Then you'll see what I mean."

Once more Jean left him alone, but this time it was different. Something good was happening, she felt. But who had sent him that book? She went through a list in her own mind, but no one really popped out. Who might have cared enough to do it and then to remain anonymous?

### Dennis

As soon as he got the news from Gwen Harper that Bob Pearson was having what Dennis interpreted as a nervous breakdown and wouldn't be back any time soon, he decided to make his move. He called an emergency meeting between the sales department and the production department to discuss what should be done in the light of the latest sales figures. He made it sound as though he and Bob had planned the meeting beforehand for this date, and that even though he couldn't be present, Bob nevertheless had given his blessing for the meeting to go ahead as planned.

Gwen Harper, of course, knew otherwise but kept silent and remained as invisible as possible. She would, however, take very careful minutes of the meeting. Dennis did not know that she knew so much about what was going on; he had always been somewhat oblivious with regard to her.

Monty Fisk vehemently protested about having the meeting at all, contending that the meeting was all one-sided since Mr. Pearson was really the person who directed the production side of the business, and he was not there to provide the strategic point of view.

Of course, Monty knew he was being set up by Dennis and that Dennis was out to get him this time. He knew his position was precarious without Bob Pearson there. His protests were in vain, however, and the meeting was fixed for later that same day.

Dennis had made a point of quietly appointing two or three loud-mouthed sales people he could rely on to spike the meeting with strong complaints. They would groan loudly about how production could never adequately service the contracts that the sales force created which meant complaints from customers and many lost sales.

He encouraged them to be as vociferous in their criticism of Monty Fisk as they liked and to point out, in no uncertain manner, how he refused to modernize and seemed unable to bring the company into the twenty-first century. That way, Dennis could stay above the fray, appearing to be only chairing the meeting, and, as usual, looking good.

Dennis began amicably, saying that the meeting was to be open and exploratory, without finger pointing on either side. The aim was to see why the figures were down even though the economy was up and to have some discussion about ways of improving performance. But he knew he could depend on his sales staff to make trouble, since most of them had been against the production staff for many years. He knew they would be calling for blood.

It turned ugly very quickly, and the finger pointing started. And they all pointed at Monty Fisk. Monty knew then that, without Bob Pearson there, he was going to be "hung, drawn, and quartered" by everyone, including, it has to be said, some of his own staff who, seeing the way the wind was blowing, chose to support the winning side.

Monty was cornered and he knew it. He tried to rescue the situation by referring to plans that were in the works to improve production performance, a good many of which were already on Bob Pearson's desk awaiting his approval. He asked Dennis to adjourn the meeting pending the review of those plans.

Knowing that the damage was already done, Dennis graciously agreed and brought the meeting to a close but not before an agreed statement of outcome was ratified that deplored the current situation and recognized the need for drastic action on the part of the production side to modernize and improve all systems as a matter of urgency. Nobody actually said as much, but the inference

169

was that Monty was the problem and should be replaced. It was a bad day for Monty Fisk. Gwen Harper couldn't help feeling sorry for him in spite of her own dislike. She could feel his loneliness and desperation and despised Dennis for setting Monty up the way he had. Meg, when she heard, felt much the same. Dennis, on the other hand, gloated. He'd had a good day.

### Bob

Later that evening, Bob reluctantly relinquished the book to Jean, but only so she could read the first chapter, he was quick to point out. He was already two-thirds of the way through and wanted to finish it as soon as Jean had read at least some of it. However, by the time Jean had covered just a few pages, he had once again fallen into a deep, but now apparently restful sleep which was to last the whole night.

So Jean kept on reading and, like Bob, found the book to be both enlightening and at the same time disturbing. She was able to see how it related to both their lives. It started to give meaning to a number of things that had happened in their lives which, up until that moment, had seemed to both Bob and Jean, totally random and without any real meaning. According to this book, everything that happens has meaning and purpose and nothing is an accident.

To Jean, this was mind-blowing stuff. As she read on, she began to see how Bob had a pattern of creating failure over and over in his life, and that this latest episode was simply another repeat of the same thing. She also began to realize that the purpose of this breakdown was to heal something deep within himself that had caused him to keep failing virtually every five years.

Her eyes became heavy and soon she was lying beside her husband in as deep a sleep as he. But even as they slept, something was happening within them both.

Bob was awake early, at more or less his usual time. He went downstairs to make some coffee and took the book with him. By seven o'clock, he had completely finished it.

He went to his study, turned on the computer, and went straight to the web site given in the book. He logged into the online forgiveness worksheet, ready to try the process that was supposed to work almost instantaneously.

But whom to forgive? He remembered the e-mail that had come only a couple of days ago. Well, he thought, why NOT Rick Tanner? Bob still had pain around that event even though it was many years ago. He would like to be free of it, for sure.

This form of forgiveness — Radical Forgiveness — was so different from traditional forgiveness that it really bore no relation to anything he had hitherto understood as forgiveness. So perhaps it might work with Rick Tanner. "Unlike traditional forgiveness, it is supposed to work almost instantaneously, so I'll soon find out," he reasoned to himself.

Bob spent the next hour and a half doing the online worksheet around Rick and the betrayal that he felt had occurred. The worksheet required that he write the story

171

of what happened, to be the "victim" fully and to feel the feelings associated with the situation.

Bob certainly was able to feel the anger and hurt, and he could feel the pain in his chest just like he had when that e-mail had arrived from Rick. But as he progressed through the worksheet, the pain in his chest subsided and the anger seemed to dissipate.

By the end of it, Bob felt more peaceful than he had in years. The pain was gone. Something had shifted in him and yet he didn't know what had shifted or why. It was a weird feeling. In response to a bunch of statements, he'd answered "willing," "open," "skeptical," or "unwilling" *(to accept),* but had not done much more than that. "How could that have changed things so drastically?" he thought to himself. Just then Jean walked slowly down the stairs and came towards him.

"It's OK, Honey," he said quietly. "It's over. I'm on the mend. But, you know, I don't mean that in the sense of it's being business as usual. I have changed, and it feels good. I don't know what it means, but the whole world looks different to me now."

"I think I know what you mean," she whispered as she held him to her in a tender embrace. "I read a lot of the book myself last night as you slept. It's going to change both our lives."

"It's already changed mine," said Bob. "This morning, I went online and did a forgiveness worksheet on Rick Tanner. I'm not saying I like him any more than I did before, but the pain has gone. The betrayal — well, strangely enough, it doesn't seem like a betrayal any more. It seems like there was a higher purpose in it somehow; it's hard to explain."

"You don't have to," she replied. "I think I understand. After breakfast, I would like to do one for myself. There are a few people I need to forgive, too."

Later that morning, Bob put in a call to Gwen Harper. "Hello, Gwen, I'll be in around two o'clock this afternoon. Would you cancel that meeting I'm supposed to be going to in New York on Friday of next week and book a flight to Atlanta instead for both Jean and me? We'll need to get there well before midday. We'll be there the whole weekend, so book us a flight back early on Monday morning. Thanks. See you at two."

Gwen Harper was dumbfounded. He sounded more up and alive than she'd heard him sound in years. Something had happened in the last couple of days, but she couldn't imagine what it was.

She put in a call to Monty Fisk but decided to forget to tell Dennis. She set to work preparing the minutes of the previous day's meeting so they would be ready on Bob's desk by the time he got in.

Bob came in right on time and went straight to his office. He read Mrs. Harper's report and immediately called her in. "Tell me what happened — and I want the whole story."

Bob listened carefully and fully understood what had occurred. He recognized it as an obvious ploy, not only to directly challenge his leadership, but to force Monty Fisk

173

to come to Bob and call in the favor he always felt he was owed, thereby bringing it to everyone's attention.

This was no surprise to Bob since he had always known that Dennis would make a grab for the top job if the opportunity ever cropped up. He understood that Dennis had absolutely no scruples about doing so — no matter who got hurt in the process.

Surprisingly, Bob felt neither angry, threatened nor upset. In fact he almost felt like laughing. He also found himself feeling sorry for Dennis that he should be so driven to carry out these kinds of schemes, hurting himself as well as others in the process. He made a few strategic calls and then called Dennis on the intercom.

"Hi, Dennis. I'm back. Would you come to my office please; right away?"

Dennis immediately went into shock and, for the first time in his life, was speechless. Gwen Harper had not told him that Bob was coming in today, and Dennis had convinced himself that it would be many days before Bob would return. To hear his voice strong and forceful on the phone was totally unnerving. He straightened his tie, took a deep breath and then made his way to Bob's office.

"Quite a stunt you pulled yesterday, Dennis," said Bob, leaning back in his chair, looking Dennis straight in the eye. "Well, it has cost you your job, and it might even have cost you your career."

Dennis said nothing, but went very pale. He just stared back at Bob in disbelief. This was not the Bob Pearson he knew.

"I have nothing against you personally, Dennis," Bob went on. "I only wish we could have worked together as a team, but for as long as I have known you, you have sought to create divisions within the firm purely to satisfy your own ambitions. You have soured relations between sales and production purely with the intent of undermining my position so you could jump into my shoes."

Dennis was about to protest his innocence, but Bob put up his hand and stopped him. "Did you really think I didn't know?" said Bob. "I have known all along that you would do anything to get this job away from me. You are totally transparent, Dennis.

"Because of the rifts you have caused, you have been very toxic and costly to this company, and I have grave doubts that you could ever change. I need to have people around me I can trust, Dennis, and you have given me plenty of reasons to think I can never trust you. I am therefore relieving you of your post effective immediately. We will work out a generous severance package for you in recognition of your years of service, but I need you out of here right now."

"You're firing me, Bob?" asked Dennis incredulously, leaning forward and slowly rising from his chair, unwinding like a snake about to strike.

But again, Bob was ready for him. He looked Dennis right in the eyes and shot back at him. "Yes, Dennis, you're fired. I'm sorry it has to be this way, but you brought it upon yourself. But listen to me, Dennis, and hear me good. As I said just now, this could be the end of your career — but it needn't be."

175

Bob paused, but kept looking straight at Dennis. "So long as you leave now, quietly, without making any fuss whatsoever," he continued, "I will help you get another position by giving you a decent reference. On the other hand, if you make things difficult around here — even for a day — I will see to it that you never work in this industry again. Do I make myself clear?"

Before Dennis could say anything, Bob went on. "Oh, and by the way, Dennis, I made my relationship with Monty Fisk known to the chairman right from the very start, even the bit about Monty's having tipped me off about the opening, so Monty never did have any leverage over me on that score at all. He may have thought so, just as you did, Dennis, but he really didn't. Ironic, isn't it?"

Dennis did not respond. By this time he had gone from deathly pale to deep red and purple, and he looked as if he were about to explode. All the veins in his neck were standing out, and his eyes blazed with rage. But he knew that Bob had him hooked and literally held his future in his hands, so he knew better than to say all that was right there in his throat.

"I would like you to have your office cleared and be gone by the end of the day tomorrow. That's all, Dennis. Thank you."

Bob had felt calm during the exchange and remained so even after Dennis had walked out of the office without saying a word. Bob felt he had done the right thing both for the company and for Dennis. Bob felt good, not so much at having gotten rid of Dennis but at having found his own power again. The weekend workshop he had booked himself into in Atlanta was going to be good for him, and he knew it.

It was now time to talk to Monty Fisk before the news of Dennis' removal got around. Bob wanted to be the one to break that news to Monty.

When he did so, Bob let Monty have his moment of triumph and to express his relief. Then he went on to make it very clear to Monty that everyone who needed to know about the past knew everything there was to know, and that Monty should not count on any favors from Bob, either now or in the future.

He also put Monty on notice that the plans for modernization had better be good, or he might well be the next to go. Bob also made it clear that Monty must commit to working with the new person who would be appointed as sales and marketing vice-president. He had to create synergy and cooperation or, again, face the prospect of looking for another job.

Monty left Bob's office in a total daze. He had been delighted to hear about Dennis, but was completely shaken by everything else Bob Pearson had to say. He had never heard him be so direct and truthful, and Monty was left with no doubt as to his own vulnerability. Bob had made it very clear to him that he had to shape up or face the same fate as Dennis.

# The Workshop Experience

Bob and Jean returned from Atlanta on Monday afternoon feeling great. Both of them felt revitalized and transformed by the experience. The workshop had given them and all the other participants the opportunity to go fully into their stories and to feel and express their feelings about what had happened in the past, or was happening to them now, before moving into a process of transformation around the whole thing.

Since both Rick Tanner and Dennis had brought forth betrayal issues for him, Bob told the group everything that had happened between him and those two people.

But the real work began, and his transformation came about, when he began sharing first about his dad and then his grandfather. He was given total permission to feel and express his anger around his dad which he did in a way that was both cathartic and freeing. Beneath that anger he discovered a terrible sadness that emanated from way deep down in his unconscious mind. The sadness came from knowing that the approval he so desperately needed from his father would always be denied him — because his father was incapable of giving it.

Bob finally recognized that reality and came to terms with it in a way that was totally liberating for him. He came to realize that he no longer needed anyone's approval and finally gave up his boyhood need for his father's. That was incredibly empowering for him.

He also reconnected with the grief he had repressed at age five, but was still there, about the loss of his grandfather and the guilt that was associated with not having been there when he died. Bob began to see how all of that was driving his life and how he himself was actually creating events in his life that replayed these events in symbolic form and confirmed his beliefs about himself, especially those put there by his emotionally wounded father. He came to see how he symbolically recreated, over and over again, his grandfather's death, which had occurred when Bob was five years old. Every five years he would create a death of some kind, actual or symbolic, that would result in shame and grief.

The pattern was that everything would go well for a while and then fall apart around the five-year mark. He saw how Rick Tanner had actually helped him sabotage that big opportunity so that he could remain "right" about the idea that "my world always falls apart after five years" and the one about his "never amounting to anything." Rick abandoned Bob just as surely as Bob's grandfather had done by dying, and he made Bob feel totally inadequate just as Bob's father had done.

Bob saw how he had been setting himself up again to fail with GiCo, Inc. He was in his fifth year as president and, right on cue, everything was going downhill.

He learned that, through something he came to understand as spiritual intelligence, he had even, at some deep level — and just as he had done with Rick — 'recruited' Dennis to play the betrayal card again for him. Furthermore, that it was all purposeful in leading towards Bob's healing. In other words, Dennis didn't really do anything TO him; rather, he did it FOR him.

179

Upon learning this, he felt bad about firing Dennis. When he mentioned this in the workshop, he was told that the gift always flows in both directions: that it was just as much a learning experience for Dennis as it was for Bob and that everything happens the way it should. Spiritual intelligence, it seems, always keeps things in balance. Upon learning this, he was able to let that go and to know that, in any case, he had done the right thing for the company.

What the workshop did for Bob in the short term was to totally reprogram his belief system around his core-negative belief that he would "never amount to anything" and to neutralize the idea that "everything falls apart after five years." Not only did this save Bob Pearson, but it saved the company and all those in it. There was no reason for the company to slide downhill any more.

With regard to his father, it was to take Bob a number of years before coming to a place where he could truly forgive him, but even quite soon after the workshop, he noticed a significant difference in how his father acted towards him. Slowly and almost imperceptibly over the next few years, their relationship was to become more accepting — even a bit more loving.

Strangely enough, immediately after the workshop, Bob found himself feeling the need to reconnect with Rick Tanner. All the old anger and resentment had gone, and he really had warm feelings about Rick.

Bob kept thinking how strange it was that Rick had e-mailed him on his birthday after all that time. It was almost as if this whole roller-coaster of change and incredible growth had started with that e-mail. He really felt that Rick might have been one of the most important people in his life, but didn't quite understand why. Gwen Harper, though, could probably have told him.

### Rick

The phone rang in Gwen Harper's office. Somehow she wasn't surprised to hear Rick Tanner's voice. "Hi Gwen. This is Rick. How are things over there these days?"

"Well, I don't know what you did, Rick Tanner, but it sure did have an effect. What did you do, you scoundrel?"

"Why?"

"Well, Mr. Pearson has suddenly come alive. He's a totally different person now. He's come into his power in a way I never thought possible. He sacked Dennis Barker on the spot after finding out that Dennis had tried to undermine him while he was away. He called Monty Fisk's bluff at long last and has taken charge of the firm in a way that we have never seen before. Everyone's talking about it, and frankly, everyone is really excited. They feel like they have a leader again.

"So, Rick, what the hell did you do?"

"I sent Bob a book."

"What book?"

"Oh, just a self-help book."

181

"Well, it must have been one hell of a book to create that kind of change in someone like Bob Pearson. He's not normally the kind of guy to be into self-help. He's usually so rational and practical-minded."

"It sure sounded like he needed *any* kind of help when you called me that day, Gwen. I can tell you this — he was in the dark night of his soul right then. Believe me, I know. I've been there. And when you're in that place, there's only one kind of help that's possible, Gwen, and that's spiritual help."

"Wow, you've changed, Rick Tanner. I never thought I'd hear you talking about spiritual matters. I know I haven't seen you in a while, but you seem different. What happened to you, Rick?. Was it when you and Barbara broke up?"

"Can't go into it now, Gwen. Suffice it to say, I was forced to grow up and to face myself. What I saw, I didn't like, so I set about discovering what it was about me that made me act like a jerk. I went to the same workshop that Bob went to last week, and it changed my life.

"How did you know that Mr. Pearson went to a workshop last week?" Gwen demanded to know.

"I have my sources," Rick replied.

"Well, don't quote me as one of your sources, Rick Tanner. I still don't trust you, you old fart. But, seriously, I am grateful for what you did for Mr. Pearson. It sure did seem to be exactly what was needed. I am impressed, Rick, really I am."

"I'm glad it did the trick, Gwen, but really, it wasn't me. I only followed my intuition. I was told what to do, and I did it. That's it."

Gwen put the phone down and had to wonder to herself how so much could change so radically in such a short time. In spite of it all she felt exhilarated.

### Bob

While at the workshop in Atlanta, Bob had been excited to learn that there was a way to bring a version of the new technology he had experienced to the entire company. It was called *The Quantum Energy Management System* (QEMS). He felt that it would help to mend the rift that Dennis Barker had created between the departments, restore relationships, and reinvigorate the whole company.

He had come to understand how each and every person in the company brought their core-negative beliefs, their wounds, and their unconscious grief to work with them. That's exactly what he had done.

In order to deal with that, the QEMS system installs some simple processes and tools into the corporate structure that prevent such energies taking hold. It helps an individual or group automatically dissolve whatever is coming up to be acted out.

He knew enough about Monty's background to understand now why he was giving Meg Smith such a hard time. She obviously reminded him, at some deep unconscious level, of his mother. Bob determined that he would offer to send

183

Monty to the workshop he had just attended in the hope that Monty's dynamic with his mother would be healed. Then he wouldn't keep acting it out over and over again with people like Meg.

He also decided in that moment to offer Meg the opportunity to become the QEMS Coordinator. Promotion for her was well overdue, he thought, mainly due to Monty Fisk's interference. She was caring and empathetic but at the same time could be firm and effective. She was bright and everyone respected her, so she was perfect for the job.

Bob immediately put a call in to Helen Barnes, the director of human resources, to confer with her about it. Helen concurred and agreed to let Monty Fisk know of their decision. Fortunately, Helen had someone in mind who could take Meg's place, so continuity would not be a problem for the production department.

### Meg

Meg left Bob's office in an absolute whirl. She'd had no idea why Mr. Pearson had sent for her. Monty had been stone-faced about it when he had relayed the message he'd received from Gwen Harper that Bob wanted to see her. She'd intuited that Monty knew what was about to happen, but he wasn't letting on, so Meg had no idea whether it was good or bad. However, when she had arrived at Gwen Harper's desk, Gwen winked at her and let Meg know by her expression that all was well as she ushered Meg into Bob's office.

Meg stood outside Bob's office looking at the pack of information he had just given her. She was to become the coordinator of this new employee development system? Although Bob had tried to explain it all to her, she really had not taken it in and did not have a grasp of what she was being promoted into. However, she had certainly grasped the fact that at last she would be free of Monty Fisk. She also felt very good about the fact that she would be earning quite a bit more money.

"Congratulations, my dear," purred Gwen knowingly. Since her conversation with Rick, she now knew that the events of the last few days, including Meg's promotion, were the result of her fateful decision to put that call in to Rick Tanner. Exactly how it had all transpired, other than the fact that Rick had sent Bob that book, she didn't really know, but she was ready to take credit for being the one to start the whole thing. "You deserve it, Meg."

"Did you have something to do with this, Mrs. Harper?" asked Meg, recalling their lunchtime conversation only a few days back.

"Not really," replied Gwen. "If I did anything at all, it was only tangentially. No, Mr. Pearson made the decision entirely on his own and then conferred with Helen Barnes, who agreed immediately."

"What about Mr. Fisk?" Meg wondered out loud. "I wonder how he'll take it?"

"Don't worry about Monty Fisk," replied Gwen, somewhat gleefully. "Mr. Pearson had him in there a while ago, and I think he took the wind right out of Monty's sails. Monty

185

came out of that office with his tail between his legs. I don't think he'll be giving you any more grief from now on."

Meg walked into Monty's office. "Congratulations, Meg," he told her. "I hear you're moving into the human resources department, and that it's a promotion, right?"

"That's right. They have actually created a new post for me, but as yet, I don't fully understand what it entails," replied Meg, unable to read where Monty was coming from or how he felt about the situation. It was as if they were dancing around each other, like a couple of Aikido fighters, each one waiting for the other to make a move. There was a long pause.

"I'm pleased for you, Meg," Monty finally said, without meeting her eyes. "I'll miss you."

"Thanks," said Meg quietly, not knowing what else to say, and she left the room. She was quite sure, however, that her dance with Monty Fisk was not yet over, not by a long shot.

### Bob

Bob decided that he would call a meeting of the whole company the next day. He would use it to formally announce Dennis Barker's departure, introduce the idea of bringing in the new energy management system, announce Meg's appointment as the program coordinator, and explain why he felt this was necessary for the ongoing health of GiCo, Inc.

He wanted to use the meeting to launch his new vision for the company and to firmly establish his leadership once and for all. When Bob walked into the meeting, he felt strong, determined and excited, better than he had felt for years.

"Good morning everyone. I don't intend to keep you long, but I have called this meeting to personally bring you up to date on what has happened in the last week or so, to share some plans with you, and to give you some assurances about our future. As you may already have heard, Dennis Barker has left the company after a successful tenure as vice president of sales and marketing, and we have retained an executive search company to find a replacement for him. In the meantime, Jim Baker has agreed to step in as acting vice-president, and I know you will give him your total support. Thank you, Jim. We are certainly sorry to see Dennis go and wish to express our gratitude for his long and valuable service to this company, and we genuinely wish him well as he moves on to new horizons.

" At this time I would like to update you on the new course that I am setting for the company — not only towards greater growth and development but with a clear vision of how we should achieve that in the best possible way for all concerned. We have some exciting new plans for modernizing the production department which we will be laying before you within a couple of months and asking for your input.

"I can share with you that I recently went through a very difficult time — personally — as we all do. However, I was fortunate enough to find a program that helped me see what was going on in my life that needed to change, not only at home, but at work too.

"As I thought about my work and how this company should be run, I realized that for a company to be strong, to be powerful, to be prosperous and to make a contribution, it needs to be founded on genuine teamwork. That doesn't just mean being efficient; it means supporting each other as human beings and helping each other be the best we can be — as people. People are at their best and contributing the most when they are happy and aligned with each other, and I intend for that to be a priority from now on.

"This company has suffered from interdepartmental rivalry of a very negative nature. This has caused a lot of unhappiness. I have seen enough of the subterfuge and the use of divide-and-rule tactics, and I will not tolerate that kind of behavior any more. It caused us to leak energy — human energy — and that is wasteful. Human energy is a basic resource that has to be used wisely, so when we leak human energy, we lose in every other way too. We lose morale; we lose productivity; we lose profitability; we lose markets.

"The company leaks human energy when people are not happy in their work or feel frustrated. We lose energy when we fail to promote cooperation and respect for our individual fellow worker. The single most important way that this company has been leaking energy over the last few years is through the interdepartmental conflict I have just mentioned. You all know what I am talking about.

"This kind of negative rivalry has been allowed to fester in this company for too long. In fact, I would go so far as to say that it has actually been encouraged by some managers with agendas of their own. When departments feel adversarial towards each other and seek to undermine each other, everyone loses.

"I will not tolerate this kind of thing any longer, and I need everyone to be on notice that if I see or hear of anyone engaging in this kind of behavior in the future, they will be placed on written final warning immediately. That said, of course, I am aware that no one can mandate a change of attitudes through edict, and I know that change cannot be brought about by threats or fear tactics.

I am therefore instituting some new policies and training programs to help us become an organization where people treat each other with mutual respect, openness and caring and where people feel valued for who they are and don't feel the need to put others down so they can feel OK.

"I want this to be a healthier place to work because the truth is that when everyone feels good about being here, and in tune with their fellow workers, they will give of their best and we will all win.

To that end, I am bringing in a training company that will help us make these kinds of changes over a period of six to twelve months. Everyone in the company will be involved, including myself, of course, and all the management personnel, staff and production people. If we are going to make these changes and reap the rewards, we must all be committed to the effort.

"The program they will implement will help us manage our own energy and have it be in alignment with company goals. It will help us plug the leaks and maximize everyone's contribution to the flow of productive energy throughout the firm."

Moving to a flip chart, Bob continued.

"If I can just explain this a little further — there are four main types of energy running through any company. The first is information or data. The second is materials and products. The third is money and the fourth is human energy.

"When human energy is not properly channeled or is misdirected, as in our case through interdepartmental fighting, it can block the flow of these other three here, and everyone loses. If it is properly directed, it can enhance the energy flow of the other three and everyone wins.

"This new program will help us to learn how to refine the flow of human energy not just to improve the bottom line, which it will, of course, but at the same time to make this a happier workplace for everyone.

"At the personal level, I will not be asking any of you to do anything I am not demanding of myself. I have recently taken a personal training, given by these same people, that has changed how I see my own life and how I relate to other people at home and at work.

"But the difference between this training and every other program I have experienced was that it gave me tools — tools that help me to get through the difficult moments and challenges that life throws at me that ordinarily would keep me stuck.

"Fortunately for us, the technology is equally applicable and helpful to groups of people, especially groups of people who work together. So, you will get those same tools to help you deal with problems in your own life that you would otherwise bring to work, as well as to improve your relationships at work.

"As I said, everyone will be involved, no matter where they work, because the idea is to give everyone in the company a way of working together and resolving issues that everyone understands thoroughly and can apply easily in any situation.

"In its simplest form, you might think of it as a sophisticated system of conflict resolution and prevention. It certainly is that and we shall be using it for that purpose and benefiting from it in that regard, but it is much more.

"It is, in fact, a way to create a very special form of synergy and workplace harmony such that it magnifies the productive energy of each and every individual in the company. Everyone benefits — emotionally as well as financially. I think you are going to really appreciate the results.

"I am confident that, by embracing this system, we will all come together in a wholly new way. I think it

191

will help us, not only to recapture the same kind of family atmosphere that once prevailed at this company, where everyone cared about everyone else, but to take that idea of caring to a whole new level. I want every person in this company to feel that they belong here and that this is a place where they feel supported physically, emotionally and spiritually.

"Let me be clear about this. I am not trying to recreate the past. Neither am I indulging in sentimental nostalgia about days that were part of a bygone age. Nor am I saying that in order to have a family atmosphere we need to stay the size we are now. Absolutely not. What I am talking about here is a modern, cutting-edge technique that enables us to manage our own individual energy so that we can each give of our best for the company and, at the same time, feel personally fulfilled.

"This technology can be applied to any company whatever its size and indeed, far from keeping us the size we are, I believe it will help us to become more productive and more successful and, consequently, enable us to grow and expand in a way that has not been possible in the past.

"I want the negativity of the past to fade away as soon as possible and for us now to embrace a policy of inclusion, cooperation, sharing and mutual support. This won't happen overnight — I am well aware of that. We all have learning to do and changes to make in our attitudes, ways of thinking and ways of being. But this new technology, as long as we all embrace and agree to use it, will move us in this direction.

"As an indication of our commitment to this program, Helen Barnes and I have decided to create a new management position for someone to coordinate the whole program. I am delighted to announce that we have asked Meg Smith to be that coordinator, and she has accepted the position. Monty Fisk will miss her, I am sure, but we feel that she is perfect for the job of implementing this program and training everyone to use it to the best possible advantage.

"Meg will be taking quite a bit of training in the technology, in the next week or two herself, to get thoroughly acquainted with the program and the use of the tools, and she will then be disseminating information to everyone. She will be arranging the seminars that will mark the beginning of the program and, once the program is running, will be the person we all refer to for help with using the tools as and when required. Those seminars will take place in about two months, off the premises but nearby and on the firm's time."

Bob dealt with a few more items of business and then brought the meeting to a close. After he left, the room was buzzing, everyone wondering what it was all to mean for them. They hadn't totally understood what Bob was talking about, but it didn't matter. Whatever it was, it sounded good.

One man from sales and marketing summed it up. "We've got Bob Pearson back, that's for sure. I don't know where we're going, but at least we're on the road again!"

## Rick

The phone rang at 7:45 a.m. That was not a time at which Rick was usually wide awake and lucid. "Hello," he mumbled into the mouthpiece, wondering who might be calling at this hour.

"Hi, Rick, this is Bob — Bob Pearson. Happy belated fiftieth birthday greetings. How are you?"

"Hey, Bob!" shouted Rick. "What's going on, old buddy?"

Bob was silent for a moment or two at the other end, and Rick wondered what might be coming next. "It was you, wasn't it?" said Bob Pearson quietly. "You sent me that book, Rick, didn't you?"

"I thought it might help, Bob. I didn't want to interfere, but I heard that you were in bad shape, so I did the only thing I knew to do. Did it help at all?"

"Rick, I'd like to take you up on your e-mail invitation to get together for lunch or something. What are you doing today?"

"I'm free. What time and where?" asked Rick.

They agreed on time and place and ended the conversation. Rick replaced the receiver and sank back under the covers, wondering what the day might bring. It had been a long time since he and Bob had been together, and Rick couldn't help noticing that he was feeling apprehensive about the meeting.

When Bob hadn't answered his e-mail, Rick had virtually written off all possibility of their ever healing the relationship. But when Gwen Harper had called out of the blue and told him that Bob was close to having what she thought was a nervous breakdown, he somehow understood what Bob needed. That was because, some two years prior, Rick Tanner had gone through his dark night of the soul and knew the signs. He also knew Bob Pearson well enough to know that Bob would have buried his pain and that it would take a breakdown of sorts to bring him to his senses.

Rick's dark night of the soul had come as a consequence of his creating cancer. When he was diagnosed, he had two golf-ball-sized tumors in his right lung and a smaller one in his left.

The doctors hadn't given him much of a chance, but they wanted to give him chemotherapy anyway. Rick didn't know what to do. He asked the doctors for some time to think it over. They didn't like it, but Rick always got his way.

Not long after his initial diagnosis, Rick was attending a conference. He had booked late and so was having to share a room with someone who just happened to be a doctor. He had been pretty mad about having to do that, since Rick liked his own space and was used to having everything he wanted, but he'd had no choice in the matter this time. As it happened, the doctor was hardly ever in the room, so they didn't have to interact much.

During the conference Rick was in a lot of pain and having difficulty breathing. On the second night, he awoke at about 3:00 a.m. struggling to get a breath.

His heart was racing, and he was sweating profusely. The noise and commotion he was making woke his roommate who, upon seeing Rick's condition, jumped out of bed and came over to Rick. "What's up, my friend?" he said. "Can I help you?"

All Rick could do was to point to his chest and get the words "lung cancer" out in between gasps for breath. The conference was taking place in a retreat center a long way from any hospital, and the doctor had no drugs or other tools of his profession with him since it wasn't a medical conference. In any case, he was no longer practicing regular medicine.

He put his hands over Rick's chest and held them there. Within a few moments Rick's heart slowed down and his breathing got progressively easier. After ten minutes or so, Rick settled into a deep sleep. The doctor washed his hands under cold running water and got back into bed.

When Rick awoke the next morning, the doctor was gone. All his personal things were gone too, so obviously he wasn't coming back.

"Who was that man?" Rick thought. "And what did he do to me last night? I'm feeling so much better!" He was breathing easier and he had no pain.

He even wondered whether he had dreamed the whole thing. Then he noticed an envelope on his bedside table. When he opened it and read the note, he knew he hadn't dreamt it.

*Friend,*

*I believe your tumors may have gone, at least for now. But they will come back soon if you don't soften your heart and tear down the walls you have built up around your heart. Forgive everyone and everything, especially yourself. Love heals everything.*
*The Doc*

## Two Years Later

Looking back over the two years since Bob had his dark night of the soul *(he still talked about it as simply a bout of nervous exhaustion but, really, he knew better)*, he could hardly believe the changes that had taken place at GiCo. Of course, Rick's having invested twenty-five million dollars into the company to facilitate the modernization had made things a lot easier, but even so, it had been an interesting two years.

The new program had been introduced, and Meg Smith had certainly turned out to be a great coordinator for it. She had organized the two-day training seminars that everyone had attended in groups over a period of time and had developed a sixth sense about when people might be needing to use the tools that came with it. She kept everyone motivated to use the tools for their own personal issues and for when issues looked like they might be arising in the work situation.

Bob had made it a condition that every applicant for Dennis Barker's position had to be in total agreement with the new workplace policy. He meant with regard to the way

197

working relationships were handled and fostered through the use of the new program. They also had to be committed to their own growth.

Well, Bob had found just that kind of person in John Peterson, who had turned out to be an excellent VP of sales and marketing. John had united his team very quickly and had increased sales by 24 percent in the first year and around 15 percent in the second.

Finding common cause with Monty Fisk, he and Monty together had instituted some radical changes in how the departments worked with each other. This had led to some great innovations in production technology which, of course, Rick's twenty-five million had helped to implement. Nevertheless, Bob knew that the money was secondary. It was the alignment of the human energy within and between the departments that drove the changes and made them effective.

Three of the five people in the sales department who had aligned themselves with Dennis Barker's divide-and-rule policy had left within a very short time of the new policies being introduced. Interestingly, they were the ones who had been creating the most trouble at that fateful meeting two years ago,

The other two came to be among the staunchest supporters of the new approach and had been promoted several times. One of them, Colin Smith, was now John Peterson's director in place of Jim Baker, who also had left soon after the changes. Jim simply couldn't handle the new way of operating. Colin Smith had been one of those who had made it uncomfortable for Monty at that meeting, but over the last eighteen months or so, they had become good friends.

Bob had sent Monty to the same workshop he had attended and it had worked wonders for Monty. It had helped him completely resolve his issues around his overprotective mother and to release all the core-negative beliefs about himself and life that had kept him stuck all those years.

Meg Smith also did the workshop as a prerequisite to becoming the QEMS Coordinator. In the end, she and Monty actually developed quite a close relationship.

At the first sign of any disturbance in the emotional equilibrium of his department, he would send people to Meg so she could help them with using the special tools and take a keen interest in how they fared. The supervisor that took Meg's place was an older woman, but she and Monty got on very well.

Eighteen months after the program had been implemented, Monty was offered a job as production manager of a much larger company at a considerably higher salary and had accepted it. Bob had given him a glowing testimonial, especially since he knew that the job was more suited to Monty's background and training.

Monty had done well in computerizing his production system at GiCo but this new firm was still fairly traditional in its approach and it would suit Monty much better. Much to Bob's surprise, Monty was there only six months before he met and subsequently married one of his staff.

GiCo had become stronger by far and had grown into a company employing more than two hundred people. Bob marveled at how all the people that had been resistant to the new approach from the beginning had left and been replaced by people who loved the idea and fitted right into it. Bob was quite sure that everyone in the company was now aligned with it.

Who wouldn't enjoy working for a company that was committed to the happiness and the overall mental, emotional and spiritual health of its workers? The word had gotten around, and other company leaders were asking Bob what he had done to make things so different at GiCo in just two years.

Gwen Harper was still his personal assistant and was as loyal as ever to him. She never would go and do a workshop, even when Bob offered to pay for her, but she got a lot out of the company seminars that Meg organized and sometimes ran. She had become much less reclusive and a whole lot less picky and judgmental in the last two years. People really liked her and always looked to her for advice. She remained the matriarch of the secretarial staff, of course, and continued to keep her ear to the ground for anything interesting.

Bob had heard on the grapevine that Dennis Barker had apparently done reasonably well for himself and was head of sales with another small company in a town pretty far away. Fortunately, Bob had never been asked for a reference. One would have been due since Dennis had not made any kind of a fuss leaving GiCo, as he might well have done had Bob not threatened him on that point. Bob was thankful for not having to pen a recommendation, for it would have been a difficult and delicate task.

Rick Tanner rarely came by and even then only to meet with Bob for a drink or a meal out together. He had invested his money with no strings attached and made absolutely no demands on Bob. He wanted no part in the running of the business except as a board member, and in fact, seldom ever spoke about the business. His passion lay in his work as a spiritual counselor and Radical Forgiveness coach, and, of course, he and Bob could now relate to one another on this level in a way that would have been impossible before.

Rick and Bob had spent more than three hours that first day over lunch talking about the true meaning of what had occurred for each of them over the years, in light of the philosophy given in the book Rick had sent and from what Bob had learned from the workshop he had attended. Rick had, of course, attended two of those same workshops some two years prior to Bob's doing so.

It had not been until a month or so later, and after their friendship had been totally renewed and a strong bond based on trust and mutual respect had been established, that Rick asked Bob if he could invest in GiCo, Inc., to help with the modernization. There would be no favors expected, and he'd prefer that most people not know about it. He especially didn't want Meg Smith to know that he had anything to do with the company. He felt sure that she hated him.

Mainly through Gwen Harper, Rick had discreetly kept up with how Meg Smith was doing, and he was especially interested in Caroline. One day she and Rick ran into each other in the grocery store. To his surprise she seemed pleased to see him and was in no hurry to break away. Rick suggested they go for coffee, and she accepted.

They spent some hours together catching up and talking about her new role as QEMS coordinator and his new vocation as a spiritual counselor. Naturally they found that they had a lot in common since both their careers were grounded in the same way of seeing things.

Bob was best man at their wedding six months later. Caroline was the bridesmaid. Jean Pearson organized the reception and virtually everyone from the company was there to celebrate. So was Monty Fisk.

# About the Authors

**Note:** Two of the co-authors have opted to use pseudonyms in order to protect the privacy and sensitivities of those about whom they have written. As a consequence, they have decided not to supply bios or photos.

**Ana Holub, MA:**
Ana is a counselor, author, mediator and peace educator based in Mount Shasta, CA. She teaches the joy of forgiveness, showing people how to forgive and guiding them into a direct experience of peace. Over the past twenty years, she has worked with women, men, teens, couples, prison inmates, at-risk families, non-profits, businesses, and schools.

Ana holds a BA in Peace Studies and an MA in Dispute Resolution from Pepperdine University School of Law. She is also a certified Domestic Violence counselor and Certified Radical Forgiveness coach. Her books include *The Edges Are Friendly* (poetry) and the upcoming

*Jumping into the River of Love.* She created *The Healing Power of Forgiveness* audio CD with 2 guided meditations to spread the direct experience of forgiveness and peace. She's worked for over 20 years in the field of reconciliation, teaching her clients practical skills for living boldly in harmony, strength and empowerment.

Her business name is Clear Path to Peace

Her Web Site is www.anaholub.com.

**Reverend Megan O'Connor.**

Rev. Megan is a talented and compassionate healer who walks her talk. Her life experiences coupled with the time she spent learning how Spirit works when a person gives up being a victim and learns to trust allows her to connect with individuals and groups on a personal and deep level.

She uses the gift of her healing energy and caring nature, as well as her background in holistic healthcare, to help people achieve spiritual, emotional, intellectual, and relational wellness.

In addition to being ordained as a New Thought interfaith minister by international spiritual healer Dr. Willard Fuller, and the Alliance of Divine Love, Rev. O'Connor has six years of experiences as a corporate trainer and five years of experience managing seminar logistics. She also studied metaphysics for 10 years and healed herself with the power of prayer and visualization.

Rev. O'Connor strives every day to be a clear channel for Spirit. In this way, she hopes to allow this higher energy to transform lives and contribute to the healing and enlightenment to the planet.

revmeganoconnor@gmail.com.

## Colin Tipping

Born in England in 1941, Colin was raised during the war in early post-war Britain by working-class parents. He has an elder brother and a younger sister. By his own account his parents were good people, loving and hardworking and he considers himself blessed in having had a stable and enjoyable childhood in spite of the social hardships of the time.

Even as a boy, he seemed to inspire the trust of people who needed to talk about their feelings, as they found in him a person who would listen and not judge. After a four-year stint in the Royal Air Force, he became a high school teacher and a college professor, but even then often found himself being sought after to provide counseling for people. He has three children from his first marriage, which ended in divorce after seven years. A second marriage lasted only four years but he nevertheless remained friends with both ex-wives.

He immigrated to America in 1984 and shortly thereafter became certified as a clinical hypnotherapist. He liked hypnotherapy because he concluded it speeded up the therapy by a factor of at least three.

He was not religious then and still feels 'free' of any organized religous dogma. His spirituality is essentially practical, and down to earth, simple, free and open-ended.

In 1992, he and his wife JoAnn, whom he met in Atlanta and married in 1990, created a series of healing retreats in the north Georgia mountains for people challenged with cancer. In recognizing that lack of forgiveness was a big part of the causation, they set about refining a new form of forgiveness which later was to become what is now recognized as Radical Forgiveness. Unlike traditional forgiveness, which takes many years and is universally seen as very difficult to do achieve, this had to be quick, easy to do, simple and therapy-free.

He is the author of several book and lectures worldwide. His workshops are renowned as life-changing experiences and he is increasingly in demand as a keynote speaker at expos and conferences. Those who have praised his work include John Bradshaw, Mark Victor Hanson, Caroline Myss, Neale Donald Walsch and Gregg Braden. He has no plans to retire.

# ON-LINE RESOURCES

## 1. *"Breaking Free,"*

## An On-line 21-Day Program for Forgiving Your Parents

This amazing program enables you to genuinely forgive your parents and to heal the wounds of your childhood, no matter what they were. Doing it on-line in the comfort of your own home, and at the moment of your choosing, makes it very convenient and very inexpensive.

The program is delivered to you in two parts.

**Part One:** This part of the program consists of a number of modules giving you information about how *Radical Forgiveness* works. You can take as long as you like going through these modules.

**Part Two:** When you are ready to start Part Two, i.e. 21 days of assignments, you simply click a button and off you go. You will have to make sure that you are going to be available to receive the e-mailed assignments, so you do have to pick your start time carefully. They will take roughly 45 minutes to an hour each day for the 21 days.

**Support:** If you find yourself needing emotional support at any time during the process, we have Radical Forgiveness coaches who are specifically trained to give help to people, like yourself, going through the program. This service is at additional cost to the program because it is optional. Alternatively, you might prefer to have a friend or a 'buddy' support you.

## Look What Others Have Said About This Program

"I can't begin to tell you how doing the "Breaking Free - Forgiving Your Parents" on-line workshop has improved and enhanced my life. It took a week or so after completion for me to notice how my attitude had changed towards my father. I can now speak to him on the phone without anxiety and, amazingly, he has not tried to push any of my buttons. We seem to be relating in a new, calmer and more loving manner. This is truly a blessing for me. Thank you so much!"
*Barb B., Missouri*

"After I started the program, I realized that the pattern had to do with a perceived abandonment issue I had beginning when I was 5 years old. I am thankful for being able to do this program and for the amazing results I have achieved."
*Heather D., Georgia*

I was blessed enough to do the 21 Days to Forgiving Your {arents On-line Program. I was thrilled, but still skeptical; believing that nothing would work on her, that she was beyond help and these circumstances would never change. Within three days I was seeing big shifts of energy. I have had some amazing epiphanies. Each day things change. Not always in big ways but certainly significantly. I no longer fear her. I no longer fear each and every move I make is wrong. Guilt has lifted from my shoulders in such a way that I am making huge strides in my life. Weekends here used to be a nightmare. Today is peaceful. Her face looks like it has shed twenty years of pain and suffering. I have changed so much since the beginning of this program."
*Tammy D., New Hampshire*

**Cost of the Program:** We have priced this program very competitively at $70 so thousands of people all around the world can have this extraordinary opportunity to heal with their parents. **To purchase the program go to www.radicalforgiveness.com**

# 2. *"Moving Forward"*

## An On-line, 21-day Program for Forgiving Your Partner

It is not uncommon for our chosen life partners to have characteristics that are similar to our own parent of that same sex, and then to have an uncanny ability to push the very same buttons. "You are just like my mother/ father," is a frequent charge made by one partner to the other when there is an upset.

This dynamic occurs because people will always take into their relationships any unhealed or unresolved issues they had with their parents. Their partners pick up and resonate with those issues and then unconsciously begin to act them out so that those with the original wounds can heal them. It's what we do for each other all the time, and is the underlying purpose of all relationships, even though we don't realize it.

This underscores the importance of doing the forgiveness work on your parents to make sure you don't bring unresolved energies into your current relationships. However, if you are noticing that your partner is already representing your parent of the opposite sex and pushing your buttons, you can, in fact, do the forgiveness work on him or her as an alternative to forgiving your parent. When you forgive your partner, you automatically, and at the same time, forgive your parent and heal the wound, because it's the same energy in both cases.

Forgiving one's parents is often not easy because you might not be feeling much emotional charge around the issue now that you are an adult. But if the issue is coming up now in your current relationship, then you are likely to have a whole lot of charge attached to it. That represents a great opportunity for you. It might therefore be best to do this program rather than the 'Breaking Free' program, or if you choose to do both, which is probably the best idea, to do this one first.

**Cost of Program:** This 21-day program is structured in exactly the same way as the Breaking Free program and carries the same price of $70.

## 3. "Self-Forgiveness, Self-Acceptance and Releasing Toxic Secrets"

### A 3-Part, On-line Program

This powerful program typically takes a person about seven days to go through it properly without rushing, but the results are amazing.

I am including it here as a relevant resource because it is not uncommon for people who were shamed or put down in some way in childhood, to still be carrying some negative thoughts about themselves that cause low self esteem. There may also be some guilt to be resolved and family secrets that might need to be released.

**Cost of Program:** This carries the same price as the other on-line programs of $70.

**To purchase, go to www.radicalforgiveness.com**

CPSIA information can be obtained
at www.ICGtesting.com
Printed in the USA
LVHW010559090120
642911LV00005B/186/P

9 780982 179000